Fred **ASTAIRE**

GONDOLA

HAMLYN

LONDON · NEW YORK · SYDNEY · TORONTO

Fred ASTAIRE

Benny Green

For Antoinette

endpapers:
Fred and Ginger dance the 'Cheek to Cheek' number
from *Top Hat*.

half-title page:
Fred and Rita Hayworth in *You Were Never Lovelier*.

title page:
Fred and Ginger perform the 'Waltz in Swing Time'
sequence from *Swing Time*.

contents spread:
Fred and Cyd Charisse in 'The Girl Hunt' ballet from
The Band Wagon.

First published 1979 by
The Hamlyn Publishing Group Limited

First published 1984 as a Hamlyn Gondola Book by
The Hamlyn Publishing Group Limited
London New York Sydney Toronto
Astronaut House, Feltham, Middlesex, England

Filmset in England by
Photocomp Limited, Birmingham
Printed in Italy

Contents

I Wanna Be A DANCIN' MAN

THE FIRST STEPS TO STARDOM

ON the map of the United States, at the confluence of north, south, east and west, stands the town of Omaha, Nebraska, heartland of that Middle West that Scott Fitzgerald was recalling when he wrote of 'the street lamps and sleigh bells in the frosty dark and the shadow of holly wreaths thrown by lighted windows on the snow'. Omaha was a child of the transcontinental railroad, and by the turn of the century a stranger arriving there would soon be taken by the elusive promise of the trains racketing through the night with the cargoes of pigs and grain on which the town's prosperity was built.

Fred and older sister Adele on her twelfth birthday. Already they had chalked up several years professional vaudeville experience.

By the time a visitor called Frederick Austerlitz first heard those theatrical sound-effects in 1895, Omaha had somehow contrived to increase its population to 100,000 without surrendering its small-town aura. The newcomer quickly settled down and within a year had married an attractive local girl. He seems to have been an engaging sort of character. In a surviving snapshot there he stands, dapper in a fly-fronted overcoat embellished with an outbreast ticket-pocket; the thumb of the right hand protrudes dashingly from a lower pocket, and the head is crowned with a soft hat whose indentations evoke overtones of 'Rose Marie'. The musical-comedy connotations go much further, for the Hapsburg punctilio of the pose is tempered by a curiously whimsical expression in the eyes, as though the subject is toying with thoughts of buffoonery; he might almost be one of those emissaries in mufti who flit through the plots of the goulash operettas of the period.

The hint of operatic slapstick is confirmed by the facts. Young Austerlitz, who was, like most of the Austrian male population, an officer in the Imperial army, one day failed to salute a superior who happened to be his elder brother Ernest. The consequences of this treasonable act, which included instant arrest, evidently gave him food for thought. Austerlitz took leave of his native land and never went back. In such ways have the lunacies of hereditary monarchy dictated the course of popular art.

Austerlitz, who went into the brewery business and changed his name to Astaire, used to say there were only two kinds of Austrians, rascals and musicians, and that he belonged to the second group, a claim buttressed by his piano playing and an obsessional love of the theatre. His wife, an ex-schoolteacher, soon had two children of her own to instruct: Adele, born 1897, and Fred, eighteen months later on 10 May, 1899. (For the record, some interesting chronology: of those whose careers became interdependent with Astaire's, Jerome Kern was born in 1885, Irving Berlin in 1888, Cole Porter 1892, Ira Gershwin and Howard Dietz 1896, George Gershwin 1898, Arthur Schwartz 1900; all but Porter from immigrant stock.)

Adele quickly emerged as a prodigy, a terpsichorean phenomenon who attended dancing school at the age of four and assimilated with freakish ease everything she was taught. Fred followed her as a kind of familial outrider rather than through any inclination of his own. His recollections of this period remain resolutely befogged, but the two children at least agree on the fact of his detachment:

Adele
I can remember he went to dancing school with me when we were just about four or five in Omaha, Nebraska. He tried his best. He was a little thing, a cute little boy.
Fred
I had some ballet training, but I didn't like it. I mean, I did toe-dancing, things like that. It was like a game to me.

It was a game he must have mastered very quickly, because in 1904 the Astaires took the astonishing step of breaking up a happy home in the cause of theatrical ambition. Mother took the children to New York in search of fame, while papa, like the benign patriarch of a magazine serial, stayed behind in Omaha, maintaining financial support and visiting his brood whenever possible.

The two significant things about this reckless migration, apart of course from the fact that it turned out to be justified, are that it was Adele rather than Fred in whom the family hopes were invested, and that the whole enterprise constituted a desperate financial gamble:

Adele
When we came to New York and we had been to see this dancing instructor who was going to teach us everything, little Freddie said to his father, 'Mr Alvienne is going to make a big star out of me', and I said, 'Don't be silly, that's me.' Poor little Freddie.
Fred
I know we didn't have any particular money. I know my mother had to sell her ring or something. I heard about it, but kids don't think too much about that sort of thing.

Fred at five, performing a routine learned at Claude Alvienne's dancing school on 8th Avenue, New York.

Within a year the Astaires were professional vaudevillians, making their debut at Keyport, New Jersey, with mother in constant attendance as manager and chaperone, although after a while father joined them permanently and took over managerial duties. The history of the next five years is a confusion of trains and landladies, a documentary justification for those hundreds of movie-musical montages where the names of tank towns ride up on the roaring of express trains and the applause swells and fades, swells and fades.

In Pawtucket the Astaires went down big, in Woonsocket they died a death, there among the Japanese acrobats and the performing dogs, the jugglers and the illusionists, the clowns with baggy pants and red noses, the theatre managers with even baggier pants and even redder noses. In 1906 the Keyport News had reported, 'The Astaires are the greatest child act in vaudeville', a statement whose superlatives

Fred wryly qualified a lifetime later by adding 'in Keyport'. Adele recalled, 'We lived in little hotels, fleabags, little boarding houses, and we didn't earn much money, as you can imagine. I think we got something like 150 dollars a week, but then you could do a lot with that in those days.'

There was a two-year break when bookings were hard to come by and the children went to a non-theatrical school in New Jersey. Then it was back to a dancing school in New York and the engagements soon began again.

Throughout this emergent period it was generally agreed that it was Adele who was the attraction, Adele who had star quality. A comically obtuse agent's report dated 1908 reads, 'The girl seems to have talent, but the boy can do nothing.' Five years later a theatre manager reported, 'This act didn't go over

above
1906: the Astaires make their vaudeville debut in Keyport, New Jersey. With Adele in white satin and Fred in the soon-to-be archetypal top hat and tails, they did a bride and groom act which involved dancing upon two prop wedding cakes, some 6 feet wide, 2 feet high, and complete with foot- and hand-operated bells and flashing lights.

right
Fred and Adele gain assurance, doing two circuit tours which took them to Pittsburgh, Sioux City, Des Moines, Denver, Seattle, San Francisco, Los Angeles, Salt Lake City, Minneapolis, Lincoln, Milwaukee, and their home town, Omaha.

very well with my audience. They seemed to need rehearsals because the boy tripped the girl a couple of times and once nearly fell into the footlights. Mild applause.' Three typical newspaper reports from 1914:

Washington DC
One of the best brother-and-sister acts seen here in a long time is given by Fred and Adele Astaire. The girl is superior to the boy.
Record, Boston
Fred and Adele Astaire gave a fine exhibition of whirlwind dancing, although it would be wished that the young man give up some of the blasé air which he carries constantly with him. He is too young for it and deceives none.
Free Press, Detroit
Every once in a while there comes along a performer who is really exceptional. For sheer personality and charm Adele Astaire outshines anyone who has appeared here in months.

It was with acts like these that Fred and Adele competed for the best spots on the bill. Mostly, they opened the first half: every performer's nightmare, with the audience cold and still settling themselves in their seats.

To Mrs. Chandler,
with our best wishes
Merrily Yours,
Fred and Adele Astaire
1915

Anyone who can watch Adele for ten seconds and not like her had better get terms from the nearest undertaker.

Whether or not the reviewers were being fair, their pronouncements, confirmed by bookers and managers, helped to create the myth that Fred was to a great extent dependent on his sister's superior ability. It was a myth to which Fred himself appears to have subscribed for many years, and it was to colour his attitude towards his partnership with Ginger, the most famous and most influential collaboration in dancing history. Time and again when the challenge arose of maintaining his career in splendid isolation, there arose the bogey of this chorus of preferment for Adele.

Everyone, it seemed, subscribed to it—everyone except Adele herself, who was not altogether indulging in the corrective of hindsight when she said:

It started in vaudeville when we were twelve or thirteen. We had to say we were older because there was a law. Children now can go anyplace and do anything they want, but we had to be sixteen, so we said we were older, and I noticed it when he started tapping and dancing by himself. Suddenly he began inventing things. I was more the clown. I mean I like to be funny, and I couldn't be bothered learning all those steps. Many times Freddie brought me to task by making me do over a few steps I did wrong the night before. Oh, I had it from him, don't worry.

Apart from denying it was ever possible to make Adele do anything she didn't want to do, Astaire's recollections of this period amount exclusively to anxiety:

All I can remember is my worry whether or not we could do our act properly and the floor wouldn't be too slippery and I'd fall on my ear or something. But then, the vaudeville business is difficult.

The first moment at which myth congeals into hard fact, when press puffery is replaced by hard-headed professional assessment, comes in 1916 with the recollection of Eddie Foy Junior:

First time I saw Fred Astaire was in 1916, Middle West. We were doing some shows with my father as The Seven Little Foys and we ran into him some place outside Chicago. Pop was crazy about them two kids, but he kept saying to the family, 'Now watch this little boy. Now there's a good dancer. Watch his style'. They were just old enough to come to New York, because you couldn't work on the stage in New York till you were sixteen.

It was 'Over the Top' in 1917 which occasioned the move to New York to which Foy refers, the Astaires' first venture out of vaudeville into the comparative legitimacy of Broadway revue, and the first point at which the names of the supporting players begin to become familiar to the student of theatrical history. Some of the music for 'Over the Top' had been composed by the great Malaprop of the Austro-Hungarian Empire, Sigmund Romberg. The producers were the Shuberts, that notorious brotherhood whose lack of formal education had not prevented, and had perhaps assisted them, in gaining a stranglehold on the American theatre. Once, when one of their sons was asked what he thought the Shuberts might have achieved had they gone to school, he replied with touching filial pride, 'If my father had had an education, he could have been Hitler.'

But although they produced the show, the Shuberts apparently did not entirely finance it. Adele has explained, with wicked innocence, how the leading lady, Miss Justine Johnstone, got the part: 'Justine was the star. She wasn't a great actress but she was a beautiful girl and somebody backed her in the show. We were just two little dancers.' The reference to the dazzling Miss Johnstone evokes recollections of P. G. Wodehouse, who once wrote a show for her and overheard her describing a 7,500 dollar pearl necklace as 'just something to wear while slumming'. As for Adele's description of two little dancers, it seems excessively modest in the light of The New York Globe notice:

One of the prettiest features of the show is the dancing of the two Astaires. The girl, a light, spritelike little creature, has really an exquisite floating style in her caperings, while the young man combines eccentric agility with humour.

Their success now became a chain reaction. The golden rule in the theatre is that in order to work one must be seen working, and it was during the run of 'Over the Top', which lasted for seventy-eight performances, that the impresario Charles Dillingham saw the Astaires for the first time and signed them up, on the understanding that they had first to fulfil a

Brother and sister in 1915. The season 1915-16 saw their final vaudeville tour. By now their material had matured, and under the tutelage of Mr Aurelia Coccia they devised and constantly polished a show-stopping song-and-dance act.

opposite
'Over the Top' (1917): the Astaires make Broadway and legitimate revue. They did three numbers together and had roles in comic sketches.

below
Adele in 'The Passing Show of 1918'. It was a musical extravaganza with an enormous cast. Fred's least favourite memory – the bird number with the lyric that went 'Twit-twit-twit-twit-twit-twit-twit – you'd better do your little bit bit bit . . .' is illustrated on page 153.

left
Fred, and Adele, get coverage in The American Stage during their next show, 'Apple Blossoms' (1919). They had just two dance spots, but both made a giant impact, with the Evening World declaring this 'the biggest hit they've ever made . . .'

prior commitment to the Shuberts by appearing in 'The Passing Show of 1918', a production whose subtlety is admirably conveyed by the style of the advertising handouts which the Shuberts had distributed:

THE PASSING SHOW OF 1918
It is a whale – without Jonah
**A HUGE WHIZZING
ENTERTAINMENT!**
A brilliant array of talent with
The Winter Garden's famous
WIGGLING WAVE OF WINSOME
WITCHES!!!
150 PEOPLE   2 ACTS   25 SCENES

Astaire has testified that among that wiggling wave was one winsome witch called Jessie Reed: 'I developed a crush on Jessie and would stand gaping at her like a dope.' Perhaps

he might have stood a better chance as a suitor had he not been so cruelly encumbered by the costume designers. Adele recalls:

We had very inferior parts in it, and Fred played a dancing waiter in one thing and threw a tray and things all over the place, which was rather funny, and the two of us did a number we loathed, dressed up as birds, twit, twit. Did my brother hate that!

'The Passing Show of 1918' survived for 124 performances, and indications that the focus was beginning to shift away from Adele over to Fred become apparent in the reactions of Heywood Broun:

'The Passing Show' has a gorgeous setting, good songs and a rather dull book. In an evening where there was an abundance of

'For Goodness Sake' (1922). Billed at number six, the Astaires stole the show. They were making $800 a week.

good dancing, Fred Astaire stood out. He and his partner Adele Astaire made the show pause early in the evening with a beautiful loose-limbed dance, in which the right foot never seemed to know just what the left foot was going to do, or cared either. It almost seemed as if the two young persons had been poured into the dance.

Dillingham's show, 'Apple Blossoms', opened in October 1919, marking a further advance for the partnership. For 'Over the Top' their salary had been 250 dollars, for 'The Passing Show' 350; now they progressed even further:

Adele
When we came up to see the great Mr Dillingham, practically cap in hand, he called us 'Little Freddie and Dellie', but oh, he was a

The ill-fated 'Bunch and Judy' (1922): the show impresario Dillingham wrote around Fred and Adele. Even the music of Jerome Kern (*above*) wasn't enough to lift it.

The Astaires get a page to themselves in Britain's The Play Pictorial. Over in London for the UK run of 'For Goodness Sake', now retitled 'Stop Flirting' (1923), they had an enormous personal success.

darling. It was a hot day, and I remember him mopping his head with a piece of blotting paper. And he said, 'Now, you kids, what do you expect to get a week for being in 'Apple Blossoms'? And my brother said very bravely, '500 dollars a week – excuse me, 550.' So Dillingham said, 'I can understand the fifty, but what's the 500 for?' The fifty was for our agent.

Heywood Broun referred to 'the remarkable dancing of the Astaires', and Alexander Woollcott told his readers about 'the incredibly nimble and lackadaisical Astaire named Fred. He is one of those extraordinary persons whose senses of rhythm and humor have been all mixed up, whose very muscles, of which he seems to have an extra supply, are downright facetious.'

If 'Over the Top' marks the point where Astaire graduated from the jolly coarsenesses of vaudeville into the pretensions of revue, then it was 'Apple Blossoms' which saw the line of his progress being intersected at several points by the creative artists who would one day provide him with some of his most

effective material. Arthur Schwartz and John Green, both soon to become successful song-writers, remember seeing Astaire for the first time in 'Apple Blossoms', and, most significant of all, one day during rehearsals when the regular pianist was away, the deputy was a friend of Astaire's called George Gershwin, whose first musical, 'La La Lucille', had opened and closed in the summer of that year.

Even when the team was involved in a flop, and even when the flop was of spectacular proportions, like Dillingham's next venture, 'The Love Letter', which opened in October 1921, they averted the disasters going on all around them. 'The Love Letter' folded like an old accordion after only thirty-one perform-ances, all of them dreadful, but most of the notices singled out the Astaires for unqualified praise. Fred was right when he said much later, ' "The Love Letter" was a flop, but not for Adele and me. We gained by it.' A few weeks after it closed a young emergent producer called Alex Aarons hired the partnership at 800 dollars a week to appear in 'For Goodness Sake'. Yet again the Astaires took all the notices, notably Robert Benchley's in Life:

There isn't much to say about 'For Goodness Sake' that you couldn't say about most musicals except that the Astaires are in it. When they dance everything seems brighter, and their comedy alone would be good enough to carry them through even if they were to stop dancing (which God forbid).

'For Goodness Sake' might have settled into a long run had it not been for the heat wave which ruined theatre business in 1922. The same could hardly be said for 'The Bunch and Judy', the next Astaire show, which opened that November and barely crawled into 1923, despite a score by Jerome Kern and some more flattering press clippings for the Astaire family album. 'The Bunch and Judy' was one of those unhappy concoctions whose future as a thea-trical catastrophe is obvious even during rehearsals and yet which defies the attentions of the most assiduous and ingenious professional doctors. Astaire, who has written at some length of the bitter experience of being trapped under such a heap, recalls:

It was called 'The Bunch and Judy'. It was a failure, what you'd call a flop show that didn't run long. It was difficult and it didn't deserve any more than it got. Although it was a difficult show to do, there wasn't much good music in it. It was just one of those

An ingenious publicity stunt for 'Stop Flirting'. London's streets were littered with thousands of leaflets designed to look like wallets containing ten-shilling notes. Closer examination revealed an advertisement for the show.

left
A party for the cast of 'Stop Flirting'. Harry Kendall is the front row.

below
Fred and Adele dance on the roof of the Savoy Hotel, London, in June 1923. At that time, if you were a theatre person you went on to the Savoy Grill for supper after the show.

things that you go through and try to forget as best you can.

What helped the Astaires to forget was their first trip to Britain. Aarons brought 'For Goodness Sake' to London, opening in May 1923, diluted the inscrutability of the title by altering it to 'Stop Flirting', and was thereby the instrument through which Astaire began to express what can only be described as a kind of Englishness by proxy, a demeanour more redolent of Wodehousean persiflage than the homeliness of Omaha:

The Prince of Wales and his brother George were my idols as far as knowing how to dress. I knew both of them and George was a good deal more of a close friend. He came to the show one night with a party and wanted us to come out and meet him. And the first race-horse I ever owned was in England. Jack Leach was riding at that time, and I met him and his father. His brother was the trainer Felix Leach, who trained my first horse, which I bought from a man called Sydney Beer. Jack used to say to me when my horse started running, 'You are now one of the racing swine,' and that amused me. I knew a lot of jockeys of course; we used to meet at the Piccadilly Grill.

The Astaires' eighteen-month stay in Britain consolidated their stature. Bad material or bad timing had dogged their last three American ventures, but Fred set sail for New York eager to build on their current success.

In London 'Stop Flirting' enjoyed the kind of unqualified success which usually drives theatrical hacks to the extremity of 'took the town by storm'. The Star attributed to Adele the ability 'to dance the depression out of an undertaker', while The Times, tipsy with its own hyperbole, unwittingly raised more laughs than the show's libretto by announcing that the Astaires 'typify the primal spirit of animal delight that could not restrain itself, the vitality that burst its bonds in the Garden of Eden. They are as lithe as blades of grass, as light as gossamer, as odd as golliwogs.'

One of the most popular features of the show was a certain eccentric dance which had begun to evolve during 'The Love Letter' and was now established as an Astaire trademark. Adele had been instructed by a choreographer called Teddy Royce to pose as though riding an invisible bicycle and trot round a circle roughly 20 feet in diameter: Fred says that the English called it the Oompah Trot, and that 'people would do it in ballrooms if they wanted to clown around. It was just a sort of run.'

Adele
It was an Oompah Trot. Oompah, oompah, and then they added to it: da dum da da da dum dum dum. Well, it amused people in those days. It was just a lope around. The English audiences were far more enthusiastic. They actually seemed to love you.

A British actor-dancer called Richard Dolman, who understudied Astaire in London, has left evidence of the degree to which Fred, who a few years earlier in vaudeville had been 'inventing things', was already developing into the most comprehensive strategist of the dance known to the professional stage. According to Dolman, Fred said to him one night, 'Always think of the exit. The exit's the thing that kills them. You can make your whole show by your exit.' Dolman adds, 'And of course he was right. Fred was King Exit. Do you realise that in "Stop Flirting" they had no less than fifteen dance routines, and in some cases two encores to a number, which added up to fifteen routines – and fifteen exits – in one show?'

'Stop Flirting' quickly grew into a London institution and its stars the unofficial emissaries of a musical culture of which the British, in that pre-Talkie epoch, knew very little. The production could have continued indefinitely had not Fred and Adele begun to experience faint pangs of unease at the length of time they had stayed away from home, an emotion no doubt accentuated by the way in which their lives had altered irrevocably with the death in Wernersville, Pennsylvania, of Fred Senior, an event which was to sound ironic echoes more than fifty years later, as we shall see. After eighteen months of the Oompah Trot, it seemed time to go home again.

On the last night of 'Stop Flirting' the audience, visibly moved by what it sensed to be the end of a chapter of experience, joined in all the songs, and at the final curtain an improbable addition to the score was made when cast and customers began singing 'Auld Lang Syne' at each other. Crowds in the gallery stood and shouted, 'Hurry back', and the Astaires must have sailed on the S.S. *Homeric* with mixed feelings, although comforted perhaps by the knowledge that Aarons' partner in their next escapade was to be the same Vinton Freedley who had played a juvenile role in that albatross, 'The Love Letter', and that the score for the new show was to be written by Fred's favourite among the songwriters, George Gershwin. Astaire's relationship with the Gershwins dates back to his vaudeville days. In an interview more than fifty years later, Fred was to recall how it had all begun:

I first met George in a music-publishing establishment called Remicks, where you could go to find material for your vaudeville act such as I was doing at that time with my sister. I used to go there and they would give me somebody to play the piano and demonstrate the song. Gershwin was one of the boys at that time. We used to have a lot of fun with these things; he was a good-natured kid. After a few meetings he said to me, 'Wouldn't it be great if I wrote a whole musical show and you and your sister were in it?', and I said we'd certainly be happy to do it, because he played just great. Actually, I recognised his piano ability more than I knew him as a composer at that time.

'Lady, Be Good!' then would be one of those rare moments when reality and the hoariest showbiz plot devices reach out and touch; the aspiring songplugger was indeed to write a show for his friends. The omens looked favourable, but what Astaire could hardly have realised was that his career was about to modulate to the second of its four phases, and that the process was beginning whereby his significance became as much sociological as musical.

Puttin' On THE RITZ

THE ASTAIRES MAKE THE BIG TIME

SO far Astaire's career had comprised a dizzying confusion in which production followed production without much sense of direction except for rising salaries and improved technique. Expediency and dedication had become so inextricably mingled that it is impossible to be sure what Fred actually thought at the time of misfires like 'The Love Letter'. Professionally the Astaires were advancing fast; there was no question of that, but so far they remained two people who appeared in musical comedies rather than people for whom otherwise indifferent musical comedies would always be remembered. They had taught critics, managements and audiences to watch out for them. What they were now about to do was to teach posterity to watch out for them. They were about to perform the deed which every outstanding artist eventually performs: to impose their style on events, to transcend the limitations of their material.

At which point it becomes necessary to define the nature of that material. It is, after all, vital to a perception of what Astaire represents to understand the nature of his reaction to his material. In all the analyses of Fred's art, the point has never fully been made, and often never mentioned at all, that in at least one regard other than his technical virtuosity he is unique among performers in the popular arts in the twentieth century. This uniqueness resides in his musicianship, by which is meant not merely that experience has taught him how to count the number of beats in a bar or to maintain a steady tempo, but that Astaire, alone among all his contemporaries, Crosby, Kelly and Sinatra included, has been a creative as well as an interpretive artist, and that this creativity has found expression in compositions belonging to that very school of music whose

most exalted manifestations he has helped to make famous. To put it another way, Astaire is a songwriter whose style is deeply rooted in the tradition forged by Irving Berlin, the Gershwins and others.

Of course his stature is distinctly minor, as he himself has always insisted, but it is substantial for all that. The most cursory examination of his published and recorded music reveals that if there is a sense in which aesthetically he may be said to have remained unfulfilled, it is that he has aspired always to the composition of songs in the Berlin–Gershwin–Kern tradition. This is not to say that any of his music is even remotely in the same class as masterpieces like 'Let's Face the Music and Dance' or 'The Way You Look Tonight'; the modest little daisies of Astaire's muse are dwarfed by the orchidaceous blooms of Gershwin's genius, and Berlin's, and Kern's. But dwarfed though they may be, they grow in the same soil, their shapes and colours dictated by the identical canons of form and content.

Once grasped, this fact places Astaire's entire career in a new light. He is disclosed, not just as a fortunate song-and-dance man who happened to attract the best work of the best composers, but as a passionate proselytiser on behalf of what his sensibilities tell him are outstanding works. He is saying, in effect, 'I may not be able to write songs as good as these, but at least let me draw your attention to the brilliance of those who can.'

It is the failure to understand this intimacy of relationship between Astaire and his music, and indeed the failure even to grasp the fact that there is such a thing as tradition at all in the world of songwriting, which has led so many commentators to misread some of Astaire's finest performances. For in the last reckoning these performances are of an essentially musical

The Broadway production of 'Lady, Be Good!' (1924). They played brother and sister down on their luck and forced to earn a crust singing and dancing in rich friends' homes.

'Lady, Be Good!', the Astaires' second London show. Hermione Baddeley, the actress, is worth quoting on their opening night: 'The Astaires were like automatons. They were magic, covering the stage with this terribly smooth, gorgeous rhythm bringing the best of American choreography together – we couldn't believe they were quite human.'

nature, and those members of the audience, often including professional critics, with no perceptions of music, have gazed upon the convolutions of the choreography and drawn the most crass conclusions about the significance of what is going on. Whether Astaire cares a fig about this kind of wilful ignorance, or is even aware of it, is doubtful, but the researcher into his career often encounters the most comically alarming gaffes committed by even the most venerable critics, especially during his Hollywood days.

In the meantime, it may be imagined what Astaire's emotions were on preparing to appear in the Aarons–Freedley musical of 1924, a show which marks the confluence of several disparate streams of development in the American musical theatre, and the establishment of not one but three successful partnerships. This was the first venture into management of Aarons and Freedley; it was the moment at which the Astaires became Broadway stars; and, most significant by far for the history of popular music, it was the first time the two Gershwin brothers, George and Ira, had been invited to work together on the score of a full-scale musical comedy. Both had worked on musical comedies before, but not together; they had worked together before, but not on musical comedies; they were now able to make their first tentative experiments together in relating words and music to the exigencies of plot and characterisation.

Not that there was much plot or characterisation to be found. Because 'Lady, Be Good!' has since become recognised as a watershed in the evolution of the American musical, it is too easy to assume that everything about it was wonderful. In fact, a great deal about it was so dreadful that Astaire very nearly never had anything to do with it at all. It is often forgotten that in the creative mix of the musicals of the period the central factor was not the star or the jokes, as managements persistently believed, but the music. Today everything about those clumsy vehicles has long since been forgotten – the identical twins and the bogus cops, the earls posing as college boys and the college boys posing as earls, the last-act legacies and the mistaken identities; the whole farrago is dead and buried – except the songs. Fred and Adele played Dick and Susie Trevor, a brother-and-sister dance team whose devotion to each other is not so intense that she cannot disguise herself as a Mexican widow and mislead him into being gulled by the imposture. It is hardly surprising that, during the out-of-

town run in Philadelphia, Adele, intimidated by thoughts of the more demanding judgments to come in New York, asked Fred, 'Do you think they'll stand for this tacky book?'

The extent to which they stood for it may be conveyed by the reactions of The New York Times, whose notice is one of the classic demonstrations of how to damn a leading man with faint praise:

When Adele left for England she was a graceful dancer – and she has returned not only with all her glorious grace but as a first-rate comedienne in her own right. Miss Astaire in the new piece is as charming and entertaining a musical comedy actress as the town has seen on display in many a moon. Fred Astaire too gives a good account of himself.

The New York Herald Tribune restored the balance somewhat:

Fred and Adele we salute you! Last night at the Liberty Theatre the young couple appeared at 8.30 and received a cordial greeting. At 8.45 they were applauded enthusiastically and when, at 9.15, they sang and danced 'Fascinating Rhythm' the callous Broadwayites cheered as if their favourite half-back had planted the ball behind the goal posts after an 80 yard run. Seldom has it been our pleasure to witness so heartfelt and so deserved a tribute.

'Lady, Be Good!' ran on Broadway for 330 performances, a longish run in those days, but some idea of how close it might have come to failure is illustrated by the peculiar history of its music, a history which provides yet another example of how hopelessly even the most informed people inside the theatre can misjudge the flowers of that songwriting tradition to which Astaire belongs. Among the songs Gershwin had composed for the show was one which has since been recognised as an American classic, and has even been defined as the greatest popular song ever written. It is typical of the fundamental illiteracy of the musical theatre, and the inability of its captains to assess the value of their own properties, that the ironies behind the production of 'Lady, Be Good!' should have reached such slapstick proportions.

The confusion begins early in 1924 with George Gershwin travelling home from supervision of a London production of a show of his

below and right
More memorabilia from the Astaires' London shows. It was their sophistication, their professionalism, their very slickness which won British audiences. Comedian Leslie Henson shares the honours on the 'Funny Face' programme, while Play Pictorial features the popular 'Swiss Miss' number from 'Lady, Be Good!'

left and above
Song sheets from two other great stage successes. Immediately popular, Cole Porter's 'Night and Day' was to become a classic amongst twentieth-century popular music.

opposite
The Astaires' endorsement was equally valuable on the other side of the Atlantic, with the British public being urged to try everything from toothbrushes to nerve tonics.

GOOD.. they've got to be good!

THEY'RE MILDER, FRED

TASTE BETTER, TOO!

Fred and Adele Astaire in Broadway's musical hit, "The Band Wagon"

Darn good—you'll say!

Everybody wants a mild cigarette. And when you find one that is milder and *tastes better* too—you've got a smoke! Chesterfields are so much milder that you can smoke as many as you like. Mild, ripe, sweet-tasting tobaccos — the best that money can buy. That's what it takes to make a cigarette as good as Chesterfield. And the *purest* cigarette paper!

Every Chesterfield is well-filled. Burns evenly. Smokes cool and comfortable. *They Satisfy* sums it all up!

EVERYBODY'S GETTING ON "THE BAND WAGON"

Chesterfield CIGARETTES

LIGGETT & MYERS TOBACCO CO.

CHESTERFIELD

Best wishes
Sincerely
Fred Astaire

called 'Primrose'. He was already working hard at the songs for the new show, and it so happened that one of his fellow-passengers was the financier and dilettante Otto Kahn. Gershwin played him some of the songs, and Kahn, something of a connoisseur in these affairs, showed his approval. Ira Gershwin takes up the story:

When 'Lady, Be Good!' was being prepared, Maecenas Otto Kahn was approached as a potential investor. He listened to the set-up, said it sounded like a success: therefore he wasn't interested. He helped financially only those shows which were worth doing but which must inevitably reach the point of no returns. Then either George or Aarons happened to mention that 'The Man I Love' – which Kahn had heard – would be in the new show. 'Well,' reflected Kahn, 'that's worth something. All right, put me down for ten thousand.' The following year, when he got back not only his money but a dividend greater than his investment, he wrote Aarons and Freedley thanking them for a unique experience – the first time he had ever received any return from a theatrical venture.

But Kahn's financial support was based on a false assumption; in fact 'The Man I Love' never appeared in the Broadway production, Freedley having decided that it lacked 'production value', an excellent example of the bogus science with which entrepreneurs have usually contrived to blind the artists around them. Adele later believed that the dumping of the song had been her fault:

I think I was probably too young to sing about 'The Man I Love', because even though we were old enough we looked younger. I don't know why but we did.

Ira Gershwin's explanation is certainly the correct one:

The song was tried in 'Lady, Be Good!'. It was written for Adele Astaire, and after the first week in the tryout in Philadelphia it was taken out because it seemed to slow up the show, which was really a dancing show. But Adele did it most acceptably. But the management didn't feel they needed the song, because it was a ballad and slowed things down.

So much for the percipience of the manage-ment, which could count itself fortunate that, even divested of its outstanding item, Gershwin's score was inspired enough to sustain a successful run.

Today the title song of the show is one of Astaire's most familiar vocal signatures, the first of those many songs in his career of which, years later, he had only to sing the first two bars for sentimental audiences to break into an applause which was part appreciation for the sheer pleasure that Astaire's performances had given them, part nostalgia at the thought of the lost years which the song represented for them. But in fact 'Lady, Be Good!' had never been meant for Astaire at all. Every show in those days had a character-comedian who could sustain the sub-plot and be featured in a few song-and-dance routines, usually with a female opposite number of Gilbertian amplitude. In 'Lady, Be Good!' this function was fulfilled by a well-known performer of the day who later graduated to Hollywood, Walter Catlett, and he shared a dressing-room with Astaire throughout the New York run.

Among those who developed the habit of dropping in backstage was Bing Crosby, then an obscure dance-band crooner:

Some of the Grand Dames in society used to come and catch the show, and then some of them would go upstairs to Fred's dressing room and visit him. One night, he'd finished the show and a couple of these ladies, Mrs Stuyvesant Peabody or somebody and a friend, came up to see these guys. Fred and Walter Catlett were dressing together in the room, and Catlett was in a bad humour. He'd been on the wagon for about a week and he wasn't feeling well. He was a bit testy. And one of these ladies made conversation, saying, 'Tell me, Mr Catlett, however did you get a bottle of milk way up on the sixth floor of the theatre?' And he said, 'I milked the wardrobe lady.' And Fred went under the table.

It was Catlett, portraying the shyster lawyer J. Watterson Watkins, who sang the title song nightly, asking a chorus of flappers to 'be good to me', not romantically but as a plea to connive at one of his underhanded schemes. Only later did Astaire appropriate the song and integrate it into that indefinable half-world of syncopated dalliance of which he has now become the symbol.

The other point worth noting about 'Lady, Be Good!' is that in it Astaire first began to experiment with solo dances. It was with 'The

Fred and Adele on the brink of stardom. Alan Dale's hapless criticism in the American still lives on: '[he] is an agile youth, and apparently boneless, like that nice brand of sardines.'

'Lady, Be Good!' reached London in 1926. It played the old Empire Theatre, Leicester Square, until it was pulled down to make way for a cinema. Again, they were as big a hit socially as theatrically: there were country-house parties, an invitation to view the infant Princess Elizabeth, and Prince George was a frequent visitor backstage. Fred bought an interest in several horses, a Baby Rolls, and some ruby-and-diamond waistcoat buttons.

Half of It Dearie Blues' that he worked out a dance featuring himself, one which so pleased Gershwin that the composer used to drop in and play the piano for Fred during his private rehearsals. When the show arrived in London two years later The Daily Sketch, with unusual perception, predicted a long run 'in spite of the fact that the book is one of the weakest even for a musical comedy that I can remember', and went on to describe Fred's solo dance as 'one of the biggest things of the night'. Fred's London understudy Richard Dolman provides another moment of illumination on Astaire the choreographer and dancer:

If I did something, he'd say to me, 'Do that again, what was that?' I remember once when I was understudying him I did one of the steps in the tap-dancing that he was doing. And he said, 'Do that again.' So I did, and he said, 'Do you mean to tell me that you've been watching me all this time and that's the best you can make of that step?' And I said, 'What do you mean? That's what it looks like to me.' And he said, 'Boy, you've got the beat on the wrong foot, but do it again, go on.' So I did it again and he said, 'Well, I might use it myself.'

Once again the arrival of the Astaires in London was the occasion for partisan audiences

to betray their intense excitement at being exposed to history in the making. This time, intimations that the closing night signalled the end of an era were rather less fanciful than with 'Stop Flirting', because once 'Lady, Be Good!' left London to go on its provincial tour the theatre was demolished, as Adele recalls:

They tore the house down after us; we were the last ones to play in the Empire, and on the last night the Prince of Wales was up in a box with all his friends; later we went back to his party at St James's Palace. We were the first Americans to invade England, and I think that as entertainers we were a little different from what they had seen. I know that a few years later everyone started copying the things we did.

The next Astaire enterprise was the mixture as before, Aarons and Freedley, Fred and Adele, George and Ira Gershwin. The plot was different but no less idiotic, involving stolen jewels and a pair of comic thugs, one of whom was played by Victor Moore. The score proved troublesome for the Gershwins, or rather the management proved troublesome to them. Ira has stated that during the out-of-town run the *entire* score was jettisoned and new songs written, including one whose lyric was so unusual that it later forced its way into three

anthologies of light verse and was borrowed by Dorothy Parker for a New Yorker story. For all its originality, or perhaps because of it, the lyric was not understood either by the leading man or the producer, according to Ira:

I wrote a thing called 'The Babbit and the Bromide', consisting of 'Hello, how are you', the old questions, that sort of thing. We introduced the song at Lymington, when we were on the road, and it seemed to go well at rehearsal. And the day my brother and me demonstrated the song, Fred Astaire took me aside and said, 'I know what a babbit is, but what is a bromide?' An hour later, in the hotel elevator, Freedley said to me, 'I know what a bromide is but what's a babbit?'

The show, 'Funny Face', contained another of those love songs with which Astaire will always be associated, not simply because he introduced it, but because it was tailored to fit his style. Today it is hard to realise that at the time Fred so debonairly introduced it there were those who took exception to its innocent innuendos; once again the man on the receiving end was the lyricist:

When we did 'Funny Face' and opened in Philadelphia, one of the town's top critics saw me one afternoon in the lobby of the Shubert Theatre. He stopped and asked how the changes in the show were coming along. He then wondered if I'd done anything about 'S'Wonderful, s'marvellous that you should care for me' and so forth. He said, 'What have you done about that song?' So I said, 'What *should* I have done about that song?' And he said, 'It contains an obscene phrase.' I said, 'What's obscene about it?' He said, 'You can't use the word "amorous".' I suppose he felt that feeling amorous was better scrawled and chalked than sung from a stage.

Two events occurred during the New York run of 'Funny Face' which indirectly affected the direction Fred's career was to take. The first was a sign that although it was Adele who usually scooped all the reviews, it was Fred who had grown into the more dedicated performer of the two. It is not ungallant to make the observation, since it has been made by Adele many times, but by 1927 she was being so constantly sought after by young men that, in Fred's words, 'Adele's beaus were a source of worry to her as well as to me.' Adele is evidently one of those rare creatures who can disarm all criticism without trying; even when she tells stories against herself in the most nautical language, she remains ever charming, and has taken some delight in insisting that there were times when she was perhaps a shade

opposite
'Swiss Miss', the final number in both productions of 'Lady, Be Good!'. It was a reworking of the 'run-around' routine which had gone down so well in 'Stop Flirting'.

left
Betty Compton and Fred in 'Funny Face' (1927), the Astaires' next Broadway show. The critics ransacked their clichés and Gilbert Gabriel of the Sun came up with: 'They are a sort of champagne cup of motion, those Astaires. They live, laugh and leap in a world that is all bubbles.' There were screen tests for Paramount, but plans for a film version fell apart.

above
'Hello, how are you? Howza folks? What's new? I'm great! That's good. Ha, ha! Knock wood.' Fred and Adele with Leslie Henson in the show-stopping 'The Babbitt and the Bromide' number, another version of the popular run-around routine. 'Funny Face' had reached London in 1928.

more casual than Fred in meeting her professional commitments.

The memory, however, sometimes wields its editorial powers in the most muddling of ways. This is how the brother and the sister recalled, across half a century, the notorious affair of the slug in the kisser:

Fred
The second night of one of our big hits, 'Funny Face', she arrived straight from a cocktail party, and she was half-sloshed when she entered the theatre. The stage door was waiting, because she should have been in an hour ahead, ready, but she'd been to this party celebrating the opening night. When I say she was sloshed, I mean maybe she'd had a cocktail too much, so I gave her a push and a slap in the face, saying, 'Wake up, wake up, we're on stage in fifteen minutes.' And she said, 'Oh, oh, you hit me,' or something. I remember that. You see, I had never touched her ever before, but I thought if we're going to do this show and this is our second night, she can't go on stage like this. So anyway, she rushed upstairs to get ready but they had to hold the curtain a bit, and she got on to the first number – we were on quite early in the show – and she really snapped out of it pretty

well and got through it. I remember I had to give her twenty bucks afterwards to keep her quiet. I said, 'I'm sorry I had to wake you up. Here's twenty bucks', and she loved it.

Adele
We were in 'Funny Face' and someone asked me out to a cocktail party. Now I don't usually drink. Certainly not cocktails, anyway. But I did go and have a martini and a half. Or maybe two, or maybe. . . . Anyway, I got to the theatre twenty minutes late, not too late to get dressed, but I had to rush to get into my clothes, and phew, I was feeling no pain at all. So I went out on stage to do this special dance with my brother, and I was so gay, and saying 'hello'. Fred was watching me and saying, 'What's the matter with you for heaven's sake?' You know, talking out of the side of his mouth. I said, 'Oh, everything's great.' We got off the stage and when we got off he gave me a slap in the face. I'd never known the likes of it. Certainly sobered me up. He was so upset that next day he went to Cartiers and bought me the most beautiful diamond charm for my bracelet.

The second event which occurred during 'Funny Face' was the screen test that Fred did at the request of the producer Walter Wanger,

Two more numbers from the London production of 'Funny Face'. Especially significant is 'High Hat' (*left and below left*), the first time Fred worked with an all-male, top-hatted chorus.

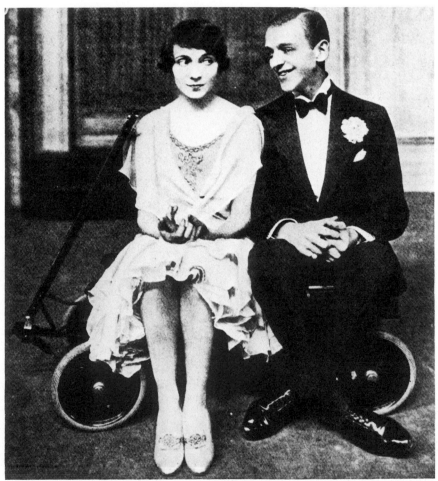

35

then with Paramount. In Fred's opinion, he and Adele looked 'awful' on screen, but Wanger disagreed and very nearly put 'Funny Face' among the pioneer musical talkies. In the meantime the great manipulator Florenz Ziegfeld turned his attention to the Astaires, who insisted on a British tour of 'Funny Face' before considering the offer.

They opened at the Prince's Theatre, 8 November, 1928, and for the third successive time in London disarmed all criticism. Among the professionals who went to see them was Sir John Gielgud:

I think he was obviously the leading spirit. As in so many partnerships, like for instance the Lunts, there was a curious feeling that the man had given the woman the feminine side of his talent, and developed it for her, and then become a wonderful partner. I always think the best dancers are the best showers-off of a woman. Obviously everyone has a kind of mixture of the two temperaments and when it comes to the dancer it's a wonderful thing.

Gielgud's reflections are perhaps the most perceptive ever made about Astaire's para-doxical status as the great master-soloist of the dance who has expressed that independence in harness with partners. But one of the concommitments of such a partnership is interdependence; when it ends through the withdrawal of one of the parties, the survivor is confronted by a major crisis of artistic identity. On the last night of the London run of 'Funny Face', at a backstage celebration, Adele was introduced to Lord Charles Cavendish, from which moment the days of the brother-and-sister act were numbered.

In the meantime there was the Ziegfeld commitment to consider, and, because the episode may be seen in retrospect as one of the funniest in all the annals of showbiz debacle, it is worth following through in all its grisly details, partly because its case history is a useful corrective to the conventional glamorous process which is supposed invariably to begin with someone saying 'let's put on a show', and partly because it is revealing to note how Fred, echoing the fatalism with which he had endured an earlier disaster, 'The Bunch and Judy', doggedly fulfilled his obligations, much as a man-about-town, on being eaten by a shark, might fastidiously adjust his necktie.

The first danger signs came with the writing of the new show. Ziegfeld had purchased an idea from Noel Coward, persuaded Louis Bromfield to 'write it out', and then hired one William McGuire to adapt it for the stage. The student of such affairs may be pardoned for wondering why, if Coward's idea was really worth pursuing, he did not pursue it himself; when a man as prolific as Coward has an idea and passes it on, the assumption is that it was not such a good idea in the first place. As for Ziegfeld's choice of Bromfield, some idea of the wisdom of that may be gauged from the observations of the critic Edmund Wilson:

Mr Bromfield used to be spoken of as one of the younger writers of promise. By the time he had brought out 'Twenty-four Hours', it was more or less generally said of him that he was definitely second-rate. Since then, by unremitting industry and a kind of stubborn integrity that seems to make it impossible for him to turn out his rubbish without thoroughly believing in it, he has gradually made his way into the fourth rank, where his place is now secure.

Having started with a mere idea and used Bromfield of all people to enlarge it, Ziegfeld now compounded the felony in his choice of

Legendary impresario Florenz Ziegfeld wanted Fred and Adele for 'Smiles', the show he was building around Marilyn Miller. Aarons, the pair's regular producer, warned, 'He won't know what to do with you.'

The Astaires with Marilyn Miller (*left*). 'Smiles' (1930) (1930) was a disaster. Fred commented that it leaned rather heavily on the storyline of 'The Belle of New York', a successful musical of the 1900s, and 'nothing seemed right from the start'.

writer-director. That he should have selected McGuire is incomprehensible, since, quite apart from any professional limitations, McGuire's personal habits, especially the odd one of taking his sustenance straight from the bottle, had already driven Ziegfeld to distraction in the recent past.

In the previous year, 1928, McGuire had found himself working on two Ziegfeld shows simultaneously. Here is an account of the affair by Charles Higham, one of Ziegfeld's less sycophantic biographers:

At least on 'Rosalie' Guy Bolton could stabilise and control McGuire, but on 'The Three Musketeers' McGuire was writing alone, and his behaviour exasperated Ziegfeld beyond endurance. McGuire was constantly being picked up in back alleys, he never had a script ready on time, and when the show went into rehearsal, he had only the first half of the first act completed. He used to rush into the office, give the secretary some wet kisses on the back of the neck, and throw some pages on to the desk.

When 'The Three Musketeers', thanks largely to McGuire's labours, began doing poor business, McGuire showed his contrition by sending Ziegfeld a wire: 'Congratulations in the darkest hour of your success.'

This was the man to whom Ziegfeld now turned in his attempts to further his love life – for one of the main reasons why he had decided to put on a show at all was to expedite his interminable courting of Marilyn Miller, the

left, bottom and opposite
Images of stardom. Fred enjoyed cars, spent a lot of time horse-racing, and played golf when he could. One thing he loathed was being asked to dance by strange ladies in nightclubs. Adele loved parties and had fun fighting off a constant supply of eligible young men.

centre
For many years Mrs Astaire was the mainstay of her children's careers. A 'gentle, soft-spoken, retiring' woman, she travelled everywhere with them, going to London in 1923 and 1926.

Ballet star Tilly Losch and Fred in 'The Beggar Waltz' number from 'The Band Wagon' (1931). He was the beggar who dreamed of performing with the star of the Vienna opera house.

unspeakable in pursuit of the intractable. Adele beautifully underplayed the melodrama when she said that Ziegfeld was 'an adorable man. I just loved him. He was as kind as could be. In those days he was rather struck with Marilyn Miller, very much.'

Miss Miller, whose literary judgment was limited, sent the Astaires a wire saying that McGuire's book was 'great'; a conflicting opinion has been offered by another member of the cast, Larry Adler:

It had a very weak story. Marilyn Miller was supposed to be a Salvation Army lass who was discovered by three foreign men—I say foreign because one had a French accent, one German, one Italian, and they had adopted

her and were bringing her up. When we started, the script was only half-finished, and I doubt that the author, McGuire, produced much more.

According to Adler, not only McGuire but also Vincent Youmans, who had composed the score, was attempting to decant himself—'Vincent used to come to rehearsals drunk. Just lay on the bench and stay drunk. I very seldom heard Vincent play the piano. If any piano playing was done, it was done by Fred Astaire and me.' The moment came when even Ziegfeld noticed that things weren't quite going according to plan. When the show reached Boston, he sent for Ring Lardner to do a rewrite job. Adler continues:

Lardner had been in Boston four days yet no progress was being made, and the only thing stopping the show was my solo. Ziegfeld said to Lardner, 'If we don't lift the book this whole show is going to be stolen by Larry Adler.' And Lardner said, 'That would be petty larceny.' Oh, it was an enormous flop. We had a salary list of 33,000 dollars a week. I don't think it ran ten weeks. [The show opened at the Ziegfeld Theatre on 18 November, 1930.] Must have lost over half a million dollars.

But the fiasco, which had been born as 'Tom, Dick and Harry', been produced as 'Smiles', and ended with the crocodile tears of its backers, was not entirely worthless. The

New Yorker praised the Astaires lavishly, the score included one of the great standard songs, 'Time on My Hands', and, most relevant of all, it included one scene which was later to become immortalised. As Adler describes it:

There was a number called 'Young Man of Manhattan'. Fred and a chorus of 24 male dancers all in white tie and tails and carrying canes would come down to the Bowery. You saw Brooklyn Bridge in the background; I was supposed to be a Bowery kid and I had a few lines of dialogue with Fred. He seemed to be contemptuous of the Bowery, so I say to him, 'Well, a lot of big judges come from here', and he says, 'Yes, and they're coming back too', meaning at that time there were a lot of trials proceeding about corrupt judges. Then we went into 'Young Man of Manhattan'. I played the mouth organ, and he used the cane as a gun and shot me and shot all the chorus boys and ended the number by dancing solo.

In his autobiography, Astaire is perfectly frank about 'Smiles', saying that it was 'the kind of flop that even made the audience look bad', and contradicts The New Yorker by insisting 'I'm afraid I was no help at all. In fact, I was ashamed of my inadequate performance.' This may be Astaire the perfectionist talking.

At any rate, Robert Benchley staggered out of 'Smiles' to announce that Fred was the greatest dancer in the world, and at least two fellow-professionals who saw the performance reacted favourably enough to want to write for the Astaires. They were the songwriting team of Arthur Schwartz and Howard Dietz, who had recently won a reputation for the creation of neat, fast-moving revues, in which sketches were relieved by memorable songs; in 1929 'The Little Show' had introduced 'I Guess I'll Have to Change My Plan' and a year later 'Three's a Crowd' had included 'Something To Remember You By'. Now they decided

'Hoops', a comedy sketch from 'The Band Wagon', had brother and sister pursuing a fat Frenchman around the revolving stage.

that the Astaires would be the perfect team to star in their new revue, 'The Band Wagon'.

Schwartz says it was Dietz's idea to recruit the Astaires, and Dietz also who thought of hanging a squeezebox round the most elegant neck on Broadway. Dietz remembers putting the idea to Fred:

He was in bed with a cold and he didn't think he could do the show. In the corner of the room was an accordion, and I asked Fred if he could play that thing, and he said he could. I said, 'I'm going to give you a tune. I want you to play that tune and no other tune on the accordion for five months', and I gave him a song that Schwartz and I wrote called 'Sweet Music to Worry the Work Away'.

Schwartz admits it was an extraordinary thing

to do to Astaire, who complained that he could hardly be expected to dance his best with such a musical millstone round his neck. Dietz, who didn't have to do the actual performance, breezily assured him that he would look good despite the handicap.

Finally the Astaires agreed to do the show, with Adele insisting it was to be her last. Cavendish, who had paid court to her in several cities, was now working in New York for a banking firm, and suitably adjacent. Adele remembers the moment of decision as follows:

Charlie was a very quiet-type person, wonderful sense of humour. I don't know how it came. I think I proposed to him. I was at The Twenty-One, which in those days was a speakeasy. I'd had one drink, because I don't

'I Love Louisa' ended the first act of 'The Band Wagon'. In the line-up (*left to right*): Tilly Losch, Fred and Adele, Frank Morgan, and Helen Broderick.

drink very much, and I said, 'Do you know, we get along so well, I think we ought to get married.' 'Right-ho', he says, and I thought no more about it. Next morning he wakes me up and he says, 'You proposed to me last night and I accepted. If you don't go through with it, I'll sue you for breach of promise.' I think that was cute.

So Fred knew, before 'The Band Wagon' opened in June 1931, that it was to be his last production with the only professional partner he had ever known. A consolation was the thought that Adele, who had always expressed a desire to quit while she was winning, was certain to do so in the light of what Schwartz and Dietz were writing.

The two partners worked intensely and with more method than their slapstick reminiscences imply. One of the special features of the revue was a revolving stage, at that time still enough of a novelty to be catered for no matter what the cost. Schwartz recalls:

We'd worked every day and almost every night for months and I was getting tired of writing songs. Howard wanted one more song to use on the merrygoround because he wanted Fred to sing while the merrygoround was in use. I said to Howard, 'We've got a song that's fine for the merrygoround called "High and Low".' 'That's a good song, we'll use it', he said, 'but it hasn't got the character I want.' We were walking together and he had his briefcase in his hand, and he grabbed a pad of yellow paper and said, 'I've got an idea.' The elevator door opened; he had one foot in it, he wrote some words and left. I looked at the words and they said, 'I love Louisa. Louisa loves me. When we rode on the merrygoround, Louisa kissed me.' Fred made it a big hit.

'The Band Wagon' is now acknowledged as one of the best revues ever seen on Broadway, not just because the Astaires excelled themselves in it, but because its score included one of the great standard songs. Memory being a cheat, most people would swear that Fred sang this song in the show; in fact he only danced it, which was unfortunate, because it was one of the very few songs in the popular repertoire which aspired to something more than the conventionalities of boy-meets-girl. It was a deliberate attempt to 'say something'. Schwartz recalls:

left
Adele marries Lord Charles Cavendish, the younger son of the Duke of Devonshire. The ceremony took place on 9 May 1932 in the private chapel of Chatsworth House in Derbyshire. Fred couldn't be there: 'The Band Wagon' was still on tour.

below
Family and professional life had to be reshaped with Adele's departure. Here, a happy retrospective: brother and sister in June 1927.

opposite
Fred, looking nothing like the 'crazy, mixed-up hoofer' he felt himself to be in the post 'Band Wagon' period.

One night at Dietz's house he said, 'I want to write a song that has more than a romantic meaning, that says something more than "darling, I love you", something about Man in existence. I don't want to be pompous about it but let's try to think of the mood of such a song.' He had a library, and it was now getting to be one o'clock in the morning, and Howard went from one book to another on

right
Cole Porter, lyricist and composer of 'The Gay Divorce', which opened on Broadway in November 1932. He subsequently wrote several film scores for Astaire: *Broadway Melody of 1940, You'll Never Get Rich*, and *Silk Stockings*.

below
With Astaire, Claire Luce: his partner in the Broadway and London productions of 'The Gay Divorce'. Her style, entirely unlike Adele's, was his inspiration for the 'Night and Day' dance. The song itself had a great success and helped what had been a very slow starter catch on.

the shelves looking for ideas for a title, and he came across a book called 'Dancers in the Dark'. 'That's it', he said. 'Dancing in the Dark. That's it.' I got his meaning immediately. I said, 'You mean that in a sense we're all dancing in the dark. I'll try to write a melody for that.' I left him and went home. It was very late and I went to the piano and I played this melody as if I'd known it all my life. It took one minute to play, and there was no music paper in the room and I thought, 'I've got to keep playing this so I won't forget it.'

Adele and Charlie had fixed their marriage to take place in England in the summer of 1932, which meant that for the post-Broadway tour of 'The Band Wagon' Fred would be working with a replacement. He has written, and there seems no reason to doubt him, that he never felt upset by the imminent loss of Adele; 'I knew I'd have to face it sooner or later.' In the past he had worried in case Adele might make a poor choice, but he knew that she and Charlie were perfectly matched:

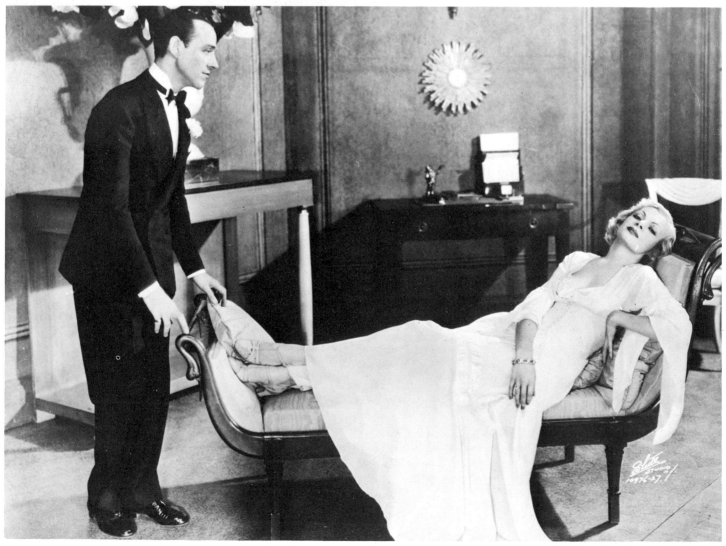

I was delighted. No, really. I don't think we ever sort of decided. She just told me she was getting married, so I didn't have anything to say about it. How did I feel? It didn't bother me because I knew it had to happen. She was certainly entitled, and I was rather anxious anyway about what I had to do myself. There was no farewell or anything like that. It was sort of, well, 'Good for you, sister, if that's the way you feel about it.'

The obvious thought which springs to mind is that Fred, who had generally been eclipsed by Adele, at least to judge from the reviews, must have wondered about his own future, whether he could sustain the impetus of his career without the asset of Adele. Adele, however, was both perceptive enough and honest enough to see that the very opposite was perhaps the case:

Well, he was a little frustrated because he didn't know exactly what he was going to do, because up to that time we were a great team. But I was the one who was pushed forward by him. If there was a laugh to be had, he'd stand back for it, that is the truth, and people wondered if he could make it alone. They thought he couldn't do without me, but the minute I left that man he went ahead. So I must have been a drawback for years, that's all I can think of.

There is little more to be said about the symbiotic relationship between brother and sister, except that Howard Dietz in his autobiography reminds us of an aspect we might easily otherwise forget:

In general Adele was more popular than Fred, but, when she told me she would shortly get married to Lord Charles Cavendish in London, I thought she should be subordinated to Fred so as not to leave too big a hole in the show. I discussed it with Mrs Astaire, their mother, who agreed.

Mrs Astaire must have been one of the longest-living as well as the best-loved parents in America; at the time of 'The Band Wagon' she had still lived out barely half her life. Her advice and opinions would continue to be respected for many years to come.

Whether or not it was pure coincidence that, at the very moment Adele took her professional departure, Fred fell in love with his future wife, is a question not nearly so easy to

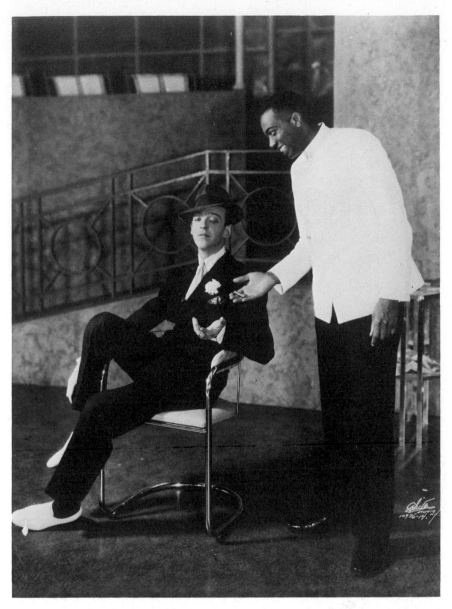

answer as a great many psychologists would insist. Fred met Phyllis Potter during the run of 'The Band Wagon', and says that she had 'so many beaus, I had to mow them down one at a time.' When he first began courting her, Phyllis had never seen Fred perform; eventually, when he persuaded her to see 'The Band Wagon' and she told him he was 'very good', he describes it as 'the most valued praise of all time'. Phyllis, who had been married before, and moved in an untheatrical orbit, was at first uncertain whether to commit herself; Fred says it was 'a tough struggle for two years', its toughness no doubt underlined by the final bowing-out of Adele, at a performance at the Illinois Theatre, Chicago, on 5 March, 1932.

Astaire agreed to appear in a new musical called 'The Gay Divorce', but before starting work on it he followed Phyllis to Europe. 'I had to make my solo before long, or else run the risk of not being in a position to marry Phyllis. It was also rather important that I

Gordon Taylor and Fred in another scene from the Broadway production of 'The Gay Divorce'.

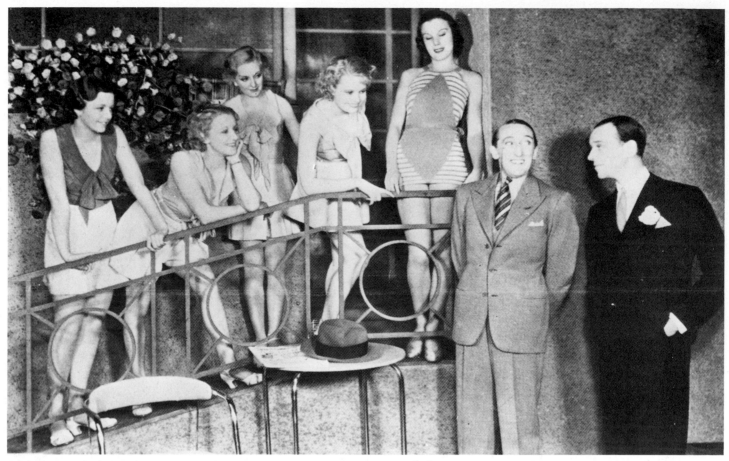

should take some prominent theatrical step quickly to counteract the problem of whether I could carry on alone or fade into oblivion without my illustrious sister.' His new partner in 'The Gay Divorce', which opened on 29 November, 1932, was an actress-dancer called Claire Luce, and in the circumstances, perhaps it is understandable that the reviewers, falling over each other in their eagerness to judge Miss Luce's viability as a surrogate Adele, quite overlooked the musical's true significance.

Astaire very quickly found that once detached from his sister he wished to detach himself from the stage generally. No doubt the discovery came as a shock to him as it did to those around him, but in an interview with Lucius Beebe in The New York Herald Tribune, he was quoted as saying:

The stage is beginning to worry me a bit. Just why I cannot say, only perhaps it's getting on my nerves, I don't know what I'm going to do about it either. I feel that I ought to dance just as long as I'm able to do it and get away with it. Lots of people seem to like it and would be disappointed if I should turn to anything else.

In retrospect it is easy enough to see what it was about the stage that was 'beginning to

worry [him].' Each stage performance is an unknown quantity; the degree of the performer's control over his part in the charade is determined by so many imponderables that no matter how conscientious or consistent he may be, he can never guarantee the quality of what he is doing. To be sure, this is one of the prime strengths of the live performance, that being live it is also unknown and therefore more exciting. However, to a perfectionist like Astaire, the greatest prize of all must be the ability to regulate every performance, to chip away a little here, add a little there, until the ultimate version of a dance is achieved. The dream had been a vain one for as long as actors had performed before audiences, but thanks to technology Astaire was to become the first great dancer in the history of the world to see the dream realised. 'The Gay Divorce' was his last stage musical.

The Boston Transcript, with brilliant perception, described Fred in the new show as 'sisterless'; The Boston Post called him 'a lone star'. The New York critics were just as uninspired:

Fred stops every now and then to look off-stage towards the wings as if he were hoping his titled sister would come out and rescue him.

Fred and his bride, Mrs Phyllis Potter, after their wedding in the Brooklyn chambers of Supreme Court Justice Selah B. Strong on 11 July 1933 (right). And the couple in more relaxed mood later the same year: in Hollywood (below right) and in London, for 'The Gay Divorce' (opposite).

We have come to the conclusion that two Astaires are better than one.

. . . a dull disappointment . . .

As an actor and singer, Astaire does not approach the perfection he achieves with his feet. He has perhaps taken on too much of a task.

So had the reviewers, who were so pre-occupied with the onerous duty of counting how many Astaires were on stage that they quite overlooked the fact that the score was by Cole Porter and included 'Night and Day', another of the songs which Astaire was to make his personal property. Even Claire Luce, who so greatly admired Fred, and evidently felt that to be selected as his partner was a professional accolade, could see very little further than the English peerage:

I felt so sorry for him. I think he missed Adele. I tried awfully hard to be as bright and cheerful as I could, and I was going through an emotional thing myself which was killing me. So I stuck that smile on and tried as hard as I could. I think both of us were going through things, you see. He had his thing, his cross to bear, though he was always very generous and kind to me, and wonderful really.

The plot of 'The Gay Divorce' was, like so many others of its kind, not worth the paper it was rotten on, and consisted of the usual dreary old farrago of divorced ladies and hired co-respondents, but any student of movies is always fascinated to learn from the cast list that among those who appeared on stage at the New York · opening were two gentlemen called Erik Rhodes and Eric Blore. The great RKO repertory company was beginning to assemble.

There is little more to say of this second phase of Astaire's career, which, by virtue of a London production of 'The Gay Divorce', slightly overlaps the opening of the third. He married Phyllis in July 1933, shared with her a one-day honeymoon and then a plane trip to the West Coast, knowing that David O. Selznick at RKO wanted him to make an appearance in a Vincent Youmans screen musical called Flying Down to Rio as soon as the 'Gay Divorce' commitment was done. For Astaire, vaguely disenchanted with a musical theatre which had claimed him literally from infancy, and deprived of the partner in whose company he had learned its every trick, Hollywood seemed like a possible source of salvation, although, like the executives sitting there out on the West Coast, he was uncon-vinced that his curiously sculpted head would look any the better for being magnified to a hundred times its normal size. Still, a man could hardly turn his back on the opportunity to investigate. So the newly-weds climbed aboard that biplane and twenty-six hours later stepped down into Hollywood sunshine. Three dimensions were about to be superceded in Astaire's professional life by two.

It Only Happens
WHEN I DANCE WITH YOU

THE PARTNERSHIP WITH GINGER

WHEN the history of popular entertainment in the twentieth century comes to be compiled, Astaire will be seen as one of the pioneers whose technique carried ancient conventions over into the new machine age. No doubt Astaire would have been a dominant figure had he been born fifty years earlier; it is hard to see how he could have failed to become one had he been born fifty years later. But being born when he was, he was in a perfect position to exploit the possibilities of a virgin medium. The vital importance of this juxtaposition of the man and the event is often overlooked in the popular arts. Crosby, for instance, happened to have the perfect style and vocal power for expression through the new-fangled microphone and the newly-perfected electric recording method; with Crosby and the new technology, sotto voce became the order of the day, and Jolson, who had been obliged to roll his eyes and shout so as to be heard at the back of the auditorium, was suddenly rendered passé.

What is interesting is that concurrently the musical comedy itself had been undergoing a vital progression of its own. In Astaire's childhood, musicals had been embellished with Ruritanian genealogies; in the year of Fred's birth the big Broadway hit had been 'The Belle of Bohemia'; the Astaires had arrived in New York in 1904 to find 'The Prince of Pilsen' playing to capacity houses; Jerome Kern, the composer who more than any other was to evolve a native American musical comedy style, and who was destined to give Astaire some of his finest melodies, had served an Edwardian apprenticeship in London and New York by having songs interpolated in shows with titles like 'The Earl and the Girl', 'The Girls of Gotenburg' and 'The King of

Cadonia', shows whose cast lists read like extracts from the Almanach de Gotha.

Throughout this period the epitome of operatic heroism was that paragon of pomposity, Count Danilo, who courted the Merry Widow with the starch of protocol crackling with his every movement, and the traditions of some impossibly venerable principality dictating his every gesture. A gentleman's profile was expected to display the same marmoreal invincibility as the heroine's bosom, which explains why, with the exception of George M. Cohan, all the lions of the American musical theatre of Astaire's boyhood had learned how to resolve a discord in the courts of the Hapsburg Empire.

Slowly a new school of composers and lyricists began to change all that. The brilliant children of immigrants like the Gershwins and the Berlins developed an indigenous songwriting style untainted either by the fustian of Mittel Europa or by the coarseness of Cohan's vaudevillian vulgarities. Astaire sauntered through a succession of stage roles as a dapper young American who dressed sharply and moved sweetly, but it was one thing to gaze on his features from the back of the stalls and quite another to gaze at them looming down from a vast screen. In Danilo terms, Astaire was a nonstarter in the hero stakes. It was technological progress which was to solve the dilemma. With the refinement of the movie camera, the mastery of the art of synchronising movement with sound, and the development of new methods of vocal amplification came mass entertainment, and with mass entertainment came the democratisation of the hero. Astaire suddenly became a viable image.

At first he seems not to have realised this; when in the mid-1920s a movie executive had seen some Astaire photographs and been told

'Heigh-Ho, the Gang's All Here' from *Dancing Lady* (1933). Guesting as himself, Fred, with Joan Crawford, performs the first of the two numbers which climax the movie, the opening of a new Broadway musical.'

53

The aerial sequence from *Flying Down to Rio* (1933), choreographed by Fred Ayres (otherwise Fred Astaire) for Hotel Atlantico's grand opening. The aviation theme was producer David Selznick's idea, but he had gone over to MGM by the time RKO finally put the film together.

that the face belonged to an aspiring movie actor, the result had been laughter in which Astaire himself had been half-inclined to join. But it soon began to dawn on him that a new era in musical history was about to open, an era in which all the old canons of taste and effectiveness were sure to be jettisoned:

I was a weird-looking character anyway and I never liked the way I photographed. And I don't think the studios did either, when they tested me in the beginning. But they got so used to it that it didn't matter. So long as you had some sort of personality that worked. That's what counted. You didn't have to be a handsome dog any more. They had had one of those handsome eras where every hero was handsome. That's not my racket.

The great film career was supposed to begin with *Flying Down to Rio* (1933), but the production hung fire for so long that in the interim Fred made his screen debut in *Dancing Lady* (also 1933), a picture with so jumbled a cast that it even included one of the critics who

had praised Fred so lavishly in Broadway days, Robert Benchley. Astaire's role in the drama was hardly arduous; he was cast as a character called 'Fred Astaire, a dancer', and was seen with Joan Crawford as his partner in a routine called 'Heigh-Ho, the Gang's All Here'.

Because this was Hollywood and not Broadway, *Dancing Lady* had four composers instead of one, including an almost indecently youthful Burton Lane:

I didn't know that Astaire was going to be in the film. There was an associate producer connected with Selznick called Johnny Constantine, and one day he invited me to a projection room to look at Astaire's test. Now I was a great fan of Astaire's. I had seen him in three or four Broadway shows and he was just the greatest entertainer I had ever seen. So seeing this test was momentous, and it was Fred dancing with some girl who wasn't up to Fred's quality, and Constantine said, 'You can get dancers like this for 75 dollars a week.' I told him this was one of the greatest talents on Broadway.

right
Fred and Ginger: a new partnership is born. Said Fred, 'Ginger was effective and she got better and better all the time. The first time she started she needed a lot of help.' And she was learning all the time: beginning to dance with her whole body, matching her hand movements to the rhythm of her feet.

below
'We'll show 'em a thing or three,' says Ginger, and they take the floor for The Carioca. Aerial acrobatics included, audiences judged this the true climax of *Flying Down to Rio*.

Lane's opinion was rapidly endorsed as soon as *Flying Down to Rio* appeared, but as to how and when the plan to pair Astaire off with Ginger Rogers was first formulated, it is impossible to reconcile conflicting testimonies. The picture was premiered in December 1933, but the Astaire–Rogers association predates it considerably. During the short run of 'Smiles', Fred had been asked by Aarons and Freedley to iron out the problems in a scene in one of their other productions:

It was 'Girl Crazy' by the Gershwins. They wanted me to help Ginger put on a little dance or something, for a song called 'Embraceable You'. That's when I first met her. I helped them put on the dance and I saw Ginger a number of times. Took her out to dinner and dancing, and that was about the limit. She was very busy.

Ginger has testified that the news that her partner in the new RKO musical was to be Astaire came as a surprise to her. She was aware that the newly-weds were trying to settle in California, and aware also that Fred was on the RKO lot. But apparently nobody had seen the two apprentices as potential partners. According to Astaire, 'I came to that studio and they said, "Oh, we must get Fred and Ginger together." You know, I didn't keep track of all that stuff, I really didn't.'

opposite
RKO put out this publicity still in the run-up to *The Gay Divorcee* (1934), Fred's third movie, describing him as 'debonnaire, dashing' and 'he of the fast-moving, twinkling toes'.

left
Guy Holden finds Mimi Glossop in a tight spot on Southampton pier. Hays Office morality demanded the title change for the film version of 'The Gay Divorce', apparently finding it easier to condone a gay divorcee.

Today *Flying Down to Rio* is remembered for the forging of the Fred-and-Ginger alliance, and for the introduction of the rhumba-style Carioca. Astaire, way down the cast list behind the likes of Dolores del Rio, Gene Raymond, Raul Roulien and Ginger herself, had so little idea of what was about to happen that once shooting was over he left for London and the European production of his

'Let's K-nock K-nees': hotel guest Betty Grable makes a play for Fred's friend, lawyer Edward Everett Horton.

The Continental

The final number in *The Gay Divorcee*, 'The Continental' was the first to win an Academy Award. And in second place? The Carioca.

opposite
'Night and Day', its pulsating rhythms are all that remain of Cole Porter's stage score.

last stage show, 'The Gay Divorce'. At which
point a telegram arrived from one Pandro S.
Berman:

At that time I was not yet in an executive
position. I was producing my own films and
didn't know anything about *Flying Down to
Rio* till it was finished. I don't think it was a
box-office smash, although it did very well.
As I recall, it was a wild and woolly picture.
It was hard to believe in all this nonsense and
dancing on the wings of aeroplanes and over
the ocean. But it had Fred and Ginger and
they gave it light.

Berman was very quickly to become the
dominating co-ordinator of the Fred-and-
Ginger production line, and among those
whose talents he utilised was a dancer with the
splendidly mythological name of Hermes Pan:

The first time I saw Fred was on *Flying Down
to Rio*, RKO, 1933. I was assigned as assistant
dance director, and that was where I first met
Fred, on a stage. He was rehearsing a routine
and the dance director asked me to ask Astaire
if he needed my help. I was terrified, because
I knew his reputation. Even then he had an
international reputation, while I was just
starting out. So I was terrified at the idea of
helping the great Astaire. He was all by
himself on the stage, going through some
routine, and I introduced myself, and he said
maybe I'd like to see what he was working
on. He was very polite and gentlemanly, as
always. He showed me this fantastic half a
routine that wasn't finished. I was awed. I
remember we got to one place and he said
'I'm up the Swanee. I need a little break or
something.' It just happened to come to me,
and I said, 'Maybe something like this', and
he said, 'That's not bad', and he used it so that
gave me confidence.

Developments followed at bewildering
speed. Astaire, who after the shooting of
Flying Down to Rio is supposed to have
remarked to Berman, 'I don't think you'll be
seeing me here any more', was informed while
in London that Berman was following him, to

THEY'RE DANCING CHEEK-TO-CHEEK AGAIN!
FRED ASTAIRE
GINGER ROGERS
TOP HAT
MUSIC AND LYRICS BY
IRVING BERLIN
WITH
EDWARD EVERETT HORTON
HELEN BRODERICK
ERIK RHODES • ERIC BLORE
Directed by MARK SANDRICH
A PANDRO S. BERMAN Production

opposite and right
Top Hat comes perhaps as near perfection as you could reasonably expect. Even Astaire, who is notably quiet about his achievements, allowed himself the following: 'I think it's a kind of standard that doesn't really age very much. It's just timeless and as long as it's going to be shown for a long time, you know it's nice to have it hold up.'

below
A publicity shot for *Swing Time* features 'The Waltz in Swing Time' number. *I Won't Dance* and *Never Gonna Dance* were earlier working titles dropped because it was feared the public might get the wrong idea about the film's content.

FRED ASTAIRE GINGER ROGERS SwingTime

THE MOST GLORIOUSLY EXCITING SHOW THAT EVER MADE A NATION'S MILLIONS TINGLE WITH SUPREME DELIGHT

with VICTOR MOORE · HELEN BRODERICK · ERIC BLORE · BETTY FURNESS · GEORGES METAXA

see 'The Gay Divorce' with a view to adapting it as a movie. Astaire was unsure what to make of it all, having been so pessimistic about *Flying Down to Rio* that he had avoided seeing it at all. Further confusion followed with a London meeting with Douglas Fairbanks Junior, who playfully asked him what he meant by revolutionising the movie industry. Astaire finally caught up with *Flying Down to Rio* in Augusta, Georgia, and found to his surprise that the experience of watching himself was enjoyable enough.

Literally overnight, and in his absence, he had become a film star. Or at least half a film star; the implications of the partnership with Ginger evidently troubled him, and he was by no means convinced that the team should be permanent. According to Berman:

He just didn't want her in *The Gay Divorcee* [1934]. First of all she wasn't English, and he said she didn't belong, which was quite true. But it didn't make any difference to me because as far as I was concerned audiences didn't give a hoot about that. Second, he didn't want to make a second picture with someone he'd just worked with. He never got over the feeling that he was being forced into being a member of a team; that was the last thing in the world he wanted.

Astaire's reasons for seeking a new partner were less personal than Berman surmised, and, not surprisingly, more technical:

Well, Ginger was a Charleston dancer when I first met her, and she hadn't had any real experience of the kind of thing we were going to do in *The Gay Divorcee*, like 'Night and Day', which I did on stage with Clair

Roberta (1935). Fred and Randolph Scott get the thumbs down from Café Russe proprietor Luis Alberni (*above*). They're selling Fred's troupe of Wabash Indianians, but Alberni won't buy – even after he's heard their 'Organ Number' (*left*).

opposite
'Manhattan Downbeat', the finale from *The Barkleys of Broadway*. Ten years on and with much of the fire gone, Fred and Ginger still got a good press but nostalgia was the keynote.

Luce, a great dancer for that sort of thing. It was just something Ginger hadn't done. By the time Ginger got into this thing she sold it beautifully.

Astaire's anxieties about the technical aspects of the partnership were perfectly understandable. He was not the only party involved who had still to realise that what was happening on screen when he and Ginger filled it was something which quite transcended the usual technical considerations. The New York Herald Tribune, in its review of *The Gay Divorcee*, stumbled closer to the truth when it pointed out that 'the photoplay gives the freshly charming Miss Rogers an opportunity to prove she's almost as perfect an example of feminine desirability in musical comedy as Myrna Loy is in drama'. That was half the truth; the other half was implied by The New York American when it described Fred as a man 'with a gay subtlety, a definite class which the screen must never allow to escape'.

After only two productions together, Astaire and Rogers had already undergone the transmutation into Fred and Ginger; they were now American archetypes, and so far as terpsichorean subtleties were concerned, Berman was right when he assumed that audiences 'didn't give a hoot'. Berman seems to have understood exactly what he was getting into from the moment he sent that first telegram to Astaire in London. 'Once I bought "The Gay Divorce" and "Roberta" and started the series, I knew it was a gold mine.'

Perhaps he did, but the time had not yet arrived when everything in an Astaire–Rogers picture was to be subordinated to the two dancers. The scripts were still feeble—the most perceptive and profound of all Astaire's critics, Arlene Croce, has said of the dialogue in *The Gay Divorcee* that it gives the impression that 'the two stars have somehow fallen among a gang of mental incompetents'; in *Roberta* (1935), which succeeded it in the sequence, RKO insured itself against what it took to be

opposite
'I'll Be Hard to Handle' from *Roberta*: a magical distillation of the essence of the Fred-and-Ginger partnership.

above
Fake Polish countess Ginger – 'you have to have a title to croon over here' – takes a lead from Fred for *Roberta*'s 'I Won't Dance' number, the prelude to Fred's longest, most virtuoso solo performance to date.

above
Irving Berlin, the brilliant composer of *Top Hat* (1935), plays 'The Piccolino'. He attended every script conference and the songs became an integral part of the film's structure.

below
The start of a love affair: Fred and Ginger shelter from the storm for 'Isn't This a Lovely Day'.

right
'Top Hat, White Tie and Tails', the second-act opener in American-dancer Fred's new London stage show.

the frailties of the dance team by buttressing the cast with Irene Dunne and Randolph Scott. But it is with *Roberta* that the transmutation of Fred and Ginger into superhuman entities is completed, and nobody could improve on Arlene Croce's description of that actual moment of consummation:

'I'll Be Hard to Handle' is the big event of the film, the number in which 'Fred and Ginger' become fixed screen deities. The wonderful secret they seemed to share in 'The Continental' becomes here a magical rapport that is sustained through three minutes of what looks like sheerest improvisation. It begins with some light banter punctuated by dance breaks, continues with music and more dance breaks–tap conversation with each other taking eight-bar 'sentences' (his growing more impudent, hers more indignant)–and ends in a chain of turns across the floor and a flop into two chairs.

Miss Croce's brief description makes clear that the Astaire–Rogers duets had already evolved into mobile character sketches, in which the theme of the plot, the pursuit of the girl by the boy and the courting of her through dance, was expressed in terpsichorean terms. It was this thematic element in the duets which rendered the partnership unique; years later, in a brilliantly astute summary of Astaire's contribution, Miss Croce suggests that 'where Astaire achieved dance films with stories, Gene Kelly made story films with dances.' The observation is substantiated the moment we take a dance like 'I'll Be Hard to Handle' and paraphrase it in literary terms. It turns out to represent, more or less, the plot of every one of the Astaire–Rogers pictures. He falls for her; she is indifferent or even hostile; he convinces her of his sincerity / attractions / affections by dancing her dizzy; she is beguiled by the sweetness of the partnership; true love dawns; end of picture.

The pair were destined to act out this musical charade several times during the decade, and the trick was achieved by virtue of a revolution in Hollywood methods which Fairbanks may well have had in mind when he playfully accused Astaire of defying all precedents. Some idea of how far films like *Roberta* were departing from conventions is gathered from the most cursory glimpse at the flowers of the

Quintessential Astaire. And to redress the balance, Fred offers this memory of Ginger's dress in the 'Cheek to Cheek' number from *Top Hat*: '. . . every time we'd get into the dance the cameramen a number of times a day would say, "Wait a minute, wait a minute, the feathers, there's a feather in Mr Astaire's ear," or something . . . and this happened so many times that we couldn't get the darn dance.'

Filming 'The Piccolino', *Top Hat*'s big production number. It's Venice and carnival time, with an overhead camera recording the revels. This son of Carioca and Continental was the last spectacular routine to come out of the RKO-Astaire stable.

previous revolution in musical methods. Astaire arrived in Hollywood just in time to witness the apotheosis of Busby Berkeley, who, in liberating the screen from the unities of time and space which had constricted the Broadway shows, had also liberated it both from the slightest observance of logical development and purely dancing virtuosity.

It is clear from the preoccupations of Hermes Pan that the Astaire–Rogers dances belonged to an entirely new tradition:

You see, in dance the better angle is to be head-on, because it distorts if you are too high, so the better angle is to be straight on. In other words you say, 'This looks great from this side, but it's nothing here.' For instance, coming forward you don't really see the effect. You see the speed. There's always something that might look great to the eye but look terrible on camera.

Astaire, with Pan as his accomplice and Rogers as his partner, was attempting, in effect, the

preservation on celluloid of the technique of dancing to music, whereas Berkeley, whose *Gold Digger* pictures were taking the industry by storm, had no interest in presenting the actual physical movements or the technical finesse and strove rather to liberate his visual effects from the age-old cage of time and space.

The audience watching Berkeley was dreaming of life in a never-never land; when it watched Fred and Ginger it was dreaming of its own existence. Given the ability to dance, most of the people in the cinemas of the world in the 1930s might have been Guy Holden or Mimi Glossop and the rest of the lovers portrayed by Fred and Ginger. This sense of identity was to have astonishing effects on the dance-hall business in the 1930s. Every man wanted to woo every lady by dancing at, with, or round her. Astaire and Rogers had succeeded in resolving the complexities of an arcane and physically demanding exercise into a truly democratic pastime. When Fred made his famous remark, 'Either the camera dances or I do', he was in effect serving notice on the doctrines of Busby Berkeley and his fellows.

At this point, with three successful colla-borations with Ginger Rogers behind him, Astaire was now about to become a figure of genuine historical significance. But there were problems, which in retrospect seem difficult to grasp. To put it briefly, RKO, for all its success with the new team, was on the brink of complete financial collapse. Berman has des-cribed how at the time Astaire turned up, 'RKO was nothing. It was in receivership. It was being run by a New York bank. We had a very second-rate company when we started. I was looking for box-office for Astaire and Rogers because I knew it was there.' It was now Berman's task, in upgrading the product, to find the capital required to do so, and in mounting the masterpieces to come he solved his problem with an almost brutal boldness.

Berman has always been something of a connoisseur of the popular composers that Astaire reveres, and the writer he now decided would be most likely to provide the right kind of music for the partnership was Irving Berlin. Berman's problem was to find a way of paying both Astaire and Berlin enough money to inspire them to work, so he negotiated on behalf of RKO, not only with his two male targets but also with himself. For *Top Hat* Astaire, Berlin and Berman were each to receive 10 per cent of the gross as their reward for the enterprise. In the event, *Top Hat* (1935) cost 650,000 dollars to make, and immediately grossed more than three million on its release.

RKO was saved, at least for the moment, Berman's fortune was assured, and Astaire and Rogers had become perhaps the best-loved boy-meets-girl team in the world.

Fred and Ginger's solo piece in 'The Piccolino'.

Helen Broderick, Ginger's best friend adds a caustic note to the proceedings. She may not always have the best lines, but she knows how to make it sound as if she does.

73

In *Top Hat* all the classic lineaments of the Fred-and-Ginger charade are mustered; in later pictures certain elements might be improved, but never was the sum of the parts to add up to so sublime a whole. Everything was fresh, the peaks were all there to be scaled, and the two stars at last had around them the three necessities: a sympathetic supporting company, an integrated musical score, and a backlog of mutual professional experience. The result was dazzling, and remains so more than forty years later.

With *Top Hat* the democratic, as distinct from ennobled, musical comedy reaches a point of perfection. Erik Rhodes, who plays the obligatory decadent European rival for Ginger's hand, and whose surface propriety is hopelessly outmanoevred by Fred's banter, is a Count Danilo come to judgement, the high-born Ruritanian shrunk to the proportions of a supernumary in the drama which thirty years earlier he might have dominated. Sleepy English eccentricity, a Wodehousean contrast with Astaire's New Yorker pep, is represented by Eric Blore. The plot, familiar to the brink of impertinence, concerns Ginger's mistaking Fred for the husband of her best friend, which gives him 101 minutes to sing and dance his way into her heart.

Which element contributes most to the success of *Top Hat*, the music or the performances, it is impossible to say, but it has long since been acknowledged that in return for his 10 per cent Irving Berlin, described by Berman as 'difficult', produced one of the most outstanding scores in the history of musical comedy. So many of the items have graduated into the pantheon of modern popular art that it is virtually impossible to regard them today with the eyes of innocence: Astaire in 'Top Hat, White Tie and Tails', gunning down the chorus boys in fond memory of an old turkey called 'Smiles'; Fred and Ginger caught in a storm in 'Isn't This a Lovely Day?'; above all 'Cheek to Cheek', one of the best-known examples of the dance song as a declaration of love.

To this day there is an element of breathless delight in the reactions of those involved, who sensed, even as they were making the picture, that something unusual was happening. Rogers has described how the film was the talk of the town because of Berlin's score. As for Astaire, the would-be songwriter and impeccable judge of quality, it goes almost without saying that he was completely overjoyed at the choice of Irving Berlin:

Astaire
I just loved his music and I was delighted when they got him to do this. And Irving thought the same about getting me to do it because he liked the way I did things.
Berlin
I never would have written 'Top Hat, White Tie and Tails' or 'Cheek to Cheek' or 'Isn't This is a Lovely Day?' if I didn't have Astaire and Rogers to write to.
Pan
It was a smash from beginning to end. It had great music, one of Berlin's greatest scores. Witty dialogue, great pace. It's one of those films where everything seemed to clinch. Just one of those strange happenings.
Astaire
I love all the songs. It was a good picture, a kind of standard that doesn't really age much. Certainly escapist, it's smart. Just sort of timeless. Acceptable at all times. It's nice to have it hold up. I've always loved that movie.

The advent of *Top Hat* is a convenient point at which to observe what happens when the American musical-comedy tradition collides with an unschooled sensibility. Most film critics are musically ignorant, which means that when confronted by musical performances they are reduced to dubious subjectives which condemn many deserving causes to neglect. In the Astaire context, it is interesting that three of the best-known writers to comment on *Top Hat* should have so utterly misread its intentions and misjudged its subtleties.

The most extraordinary reaction of all to Astaire was that of James Agate who announced the utter pointlessness of tap-dancing. It was perhaps unwise of Agate to say it even though he believed it, for if there is any enterprise more pointless than tap-dancing, it is publishing an essay which says so. But then Agate was one of millions who had no equipment by which to measure the relative merits of an Irving Berlin and any studio hack; if there is truth in the Shavian dictum that to a blind man a picture gallery is a dull place, what can a deaf one be expected to make of melodiousness? The problem is exemplified by the dilemma of Graham Greene, who, in reviewing *Top Hat* for The Spectator, said that 'it doesn't really matter much that the music and lyrics are bad', at which point the reader begins to wonder 'bad in comparison to what?' Greene goes on to compound a critical felony by describing Astaire as 'the nearest approach we are ever likely to have to a human Mickey Mouse', a

Let Yourself Go

Fred and Ginger set a
cracking pace for their
winning entry in the
Paradise Ballroom dance
contest. Vocals were
provided by Ginger, with a
backing trio which included
Betty Grable.

right
Fred and friend go
a-wooing. Fred is a hoofer-
turned-sailor who meets up
with ex-partner Ginger when
he and his cronies crash the
dance hall where she now
works.

below
Back into evening gear for
the 'Let's Face the Music'
sequence, the finale of *Follow
the Fleet* and part of the
benefit show Fred organizes
to salvage a ship. Fred had
problems with this dress too:
a clout in the eye from the
several-pounder beaded
sleeves rendered him
somewhat insensible to the
fourteen takes. Nonetheless,
critic Arlene Croce rates the
number briskly sublime.

choice of simile echoed most curiously by the
third of our distinguished prosodists, Alistair
Cooke, who, mistakenly informed that *Top
Hat* was to be the last Fred-and-Ginger film,
said in his review, 'Let's hope that when his
present partner deserts him he'll call himself by
his real name and make a new series of musicals,
partnered as God meant he should be, by his
first and oldest flame, Miss Minnie Mouse.'

Against this kind of obtuseness, it is edu-
cational to balance the reflections of Arlene
Croce on the climactic dance of the next film in
the series, *Follow the Fleet* (1936). The setting
for the song, one of the best-known of all 1930s
movies, is described by Hermes Pan:

The title 'Let's Face the Music and Dance'
suggested to us something where the girl was
unhappy and so was he, but they finally faced
the music and danced. So she was about to
jump off a cliff or something in Monte Carlo
or somewhere, and Fred has lost his money at
the gaming table and he meets her.

The song is one of Berlin's most original masterpieces, a sumptuous reproach to the trendy jackasses of a later age who were to belittle the music of the Astaire era for its refusal to venture away from the 32-bar form. Miss Croce's analysis of what happened when Astaire and Rogers interpreted Berlin's best work is worth reproducing at some length:

. . . a terrace at the top of the casino. He is elaborately shunned by society. Alone, he takes out a small pistol, but just then Rogers appears at the far side of the stage, twisting a long chiffon handkerchief and gazing out over the parapet. She steps up on it but he prevents the leap. Ruefully he shows her his empty wallet and the gun which she looks at unseeingly, then tries to snatch. He throws both away and *sings*.
How they got through all this without a laugh is their secret. The song is like one of those brave ballads of the Depression written by Schwartz and Dietz–'Dancing in the Dark' or 'Alone Together'–and the mood is awesomely grave. The dance is one of their simplest and most daring, the steps mostly walking steps done with a slight retard. The withheld impetus makes the dance look dragged by destiny, all the quick little circling steps pulled as if on a single thread. A beautiful moment occurs when he promenades her as she holds a pose on half-toe with one lifted knee. . . . What I find most moving in this noble and almost absurdly glamorous dance is the absence of self-enchantment in the performance.

That Miss Croce is right and the Mickey Mouse brigade hopelessly wrong has since been confirmed by history; 'Let's Face the Music and Dance' is one of the sequences in movie history which expresses the quintessence of the romance and sophistication for which Hollywood was always striving and so rarely achieved.

It is at least possible, however, that Astaire himself might have been embarrassed by the Crocean eulogies. His attitude towards his own

Fred and composer Johnny Green put in rehearsal time on radio's Packard Hour. The show went out every Tuesday evening on the NBC-Red network.

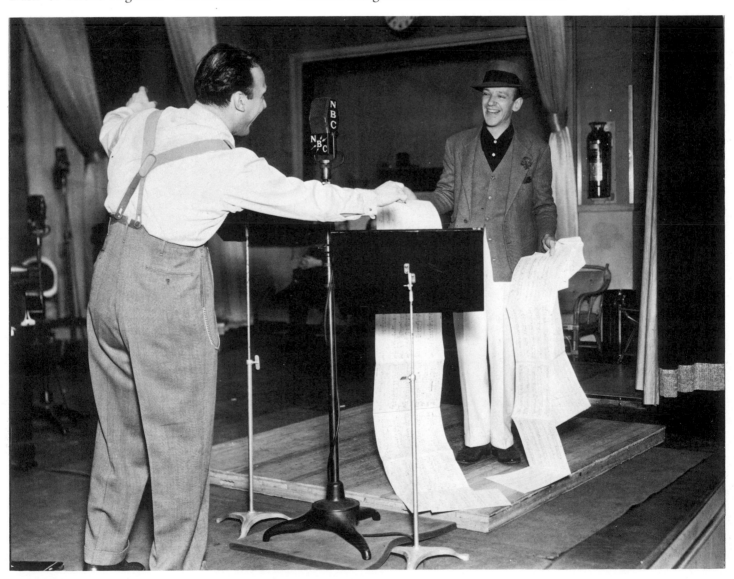

The Waltz in Swing Time

Swing Time (1936). Of this number, Arlene Croce has said, 'It is pure white: pure vision and sound.' Lasting approximately 2½ minutes, 'The Waltz in Swing Time' was shot in one take, and the result is a superbly sustained piece of romanticism.

'Never Gonna Dance'. Fred and Ginger part, supposedly for ever: all the more poignant when you recollect that *Swing Time* saw the end of the partnership's truly great period. Hermes Pan records that the last sixteen bars needed forty-seven takes and Ginger's feet were bleeding by the end of it.

dancing has always been consistently to eschew idolatry, always with the insistence that when he did his routines he was 'just doing a job'. Nowhere in the Astaire reminiscences will the researcher ever encounter the palest ghost of technical self-pride or pretentiousness, and it is typical of the man that his recollection of *Follow the Fleet*, veering starkly away from Miss Croce's justified raptures, should concentrate, almost perversely, on the smalltalk of reality. At the time the picture was being shot, Phyllis was pregnant with the child soon to be christened Fred Junior:

When he was being born, Irving was out here and I was living at the hospital and Irving used to come and play gin rummy with me every night. I've always loved the way Irving did things. He would say, 'Well, I've got a great idea for a song, kid.' There would be some show coming up, and he would throw song ideas at me to see how I liked this or that while we'd be playing gin. Well, he'd say so-and-so and I'd say, 'That sounds good. I like that.' And then he'd say, 'Gin', and lay his cards down. I don't think he did it on purpose, but he was always thinking of songs. An absolute genius.

It was around this time that Astaire's radio career began, a successful and lucrative departure which pleased everyone except the perfectionist Astaire, who was inhibited by the restriction on his movements imposed by the microphone. 'I stood there banging away at these funny little steps; it didn't interest me very much. I like to cover ground and jump over things.' The prime consideration remained the partnership with Ginger and the RKO production line.

By now, with the sixth successive Astaire–Rogers film, *Swing Time* (1936), in the pipeline, critics were able to place the performances in a context of past achievements, and although the main song from the score, 'The Way You Look Tonight', won an Academy Award for its composer and lyricist, Jerome Kern and Dorothy Fields, the general climate of opinion insisted that the best was past. Moreover, both partners appear to have been keen to assert their autonomy, especially Ginger, who was determined to express what talents she had as a dramatic actress. It was agreed, however, that before the break, the team should complete *Shall We Dance*, in which Astaire and Rogers were reunited with the music of the Gershwin brothers, George and Ira.

Swing Time notched up Fred's first, and last, blackface routine. The 'Bojangles of Harlem' number was a tribute to the great Bill 'Bojangles' Robinson, tap-dancer extraordinary. The high point comes when he dances in and out of sync with three great silhouettes of himself.

opposite
'They All Laughed': Fred and Ginger's first duet in *Shall We Dance*. Judging this the only classic Astaire-Rogers piece in the film, critic Arlene Croce sums it up with the words, 'The number has everything – games, jokes, hard tap, cool tap, a lovely series of ballet finger turns, and two white pianos to jump onto.'

below
The title number from *Shall We Dance* (1937). 'If I can't dance with one Linda, I'll dance with dozens,' declared Fred after a quarrel. His true love revealed, the real Ginger will finally rescue him from a chorus of masked dancers.

Shall We Dance (1937) had an air about it of a falling-away in romantic intensity, but it did succeed in adding a new sequence to the collection of indispensable Hollywood archetypes, the moment when Astaire, as Pete Peters, sings to Ginger, as Linda Keene, on the Hoboken ferry. It is night, and fog lingers on the waters; the mood is sad because, according to the inexplicable convolutions of the plot, the two lovers have to marry in order that they may be divorced. For this scene the Gershwins wrote one of those songs which seem to symbolise a period, 'They Can't Take That Away From Me', yet another in the catalogue of compositions which, in the years after, Fred had only to mention for audiences to break into spontaneous applause.

In spite of the film's commercial appeal, RKO now agreed to split the partnership. Ginger has described how she wanted to do 'more dramatic' roles, unaware that the most dramatic instants of her career, cinematically speaking, were to remain those intensely poignant moments bequeathed to her by men like Berlin and Gershwin. Inevitably the break-up of the most successful dancing team of the century at the peak of its popularity tempted reporters to talk of bitter feuds and even hatred. The columnist Sheilah Graham reacted against the theory:

I never believed any of it, because I knew the kind of person Fred was. I knew how devoted he was to his wife; as for disliking Ginger, they were the best team. He danced later with other girls who were better dancers than Ginger, like Cyd Charisse and Eleanor Powell and Rita Hayworth, but none of them came off like Ginger came off. She was a beautiful doll who looked innocent and very happy. The combination was terrific. Fred was never as good with anyone else, so, being a smart person, he's not an idiot. I doubt if he would allow himself to dislike Ginger.

WS-168

making of a musical picture with a co-star who neither sang nor danced. The background to *A Damsel in Distress* (1937) is an object lesson in how not to make movies; most of its history falls outside the compass of Astaire's career, except that the original novel, published by P. G. Wodehouse in 1919, attracted George Gershwin because of the coincidence that its hero is an American composer called George. The book had gone through countless script-writing hands before it finally emerged as a screenplay, and some idea of the ineptitude against which Astaire had to struggle is conveyed by Wodehouse's reminiscences:

Gershwin used his considerable influence to have it done on the screen, and it was handed over to the hired assassins who at that time were such a feature of Dottyville-on-the-Pacific. The result was a Mess which for some reason is still shown occasionally on American TV and causes sets to be switched off from the rockbound coasts of Maine to the Everglades of Florida. Friends have often commented on the dark circles beneath my eyes and my tendency to leap like a jumping bean at sudden noises, and I find those phenomena easy to explain. It is only fifty years or so since I was involved in the shooting of 'A Damsel in Distress'.

Perhaps Arlene Croce was right to suggest that the split was caused not by personal enmity but by professional pride.

At first, the break-up was to be a temporary affair, to enable all concerned to rediscover the first fine careless rapture of *Top Hat*. Ginger went off to do *Stage Door* with Katharine Hepburn, while Fred became committed to what remains the most incomprehensible sequence of events in his entire career, the

The Manglers, as the official term was, proved worthy of the trust placed in them by the studio. The first thing they did was eliminate the story and substitute for it one more suitable to retarded adults and children with water on the brain. Then they turned their attention to the hero. There was not much they could do here, but they did their best by engaging Fred Astaire and giving him nobody to dance with, so that he had nine solo numbers. To a jaundiced eye it seemed there was not a moment when he was not on the screen by himself, singing and dancing his heart out, with nobody to lend him a helping hand.

Wodehouse's strictures are utterly justified, but his claim that nobody wants to see the picture is not; its score included 'A Foggy Day', a fact which has probably saved it from oblivion. Nobody ever had any illusions about the clumsiness of the production, and Astaire has told how his leading lady brought to her task, at least in retrospect, a degree of realism sadly lacking in the moguls' responsibility for Wodehouse's 'Mess'.

Joan Fontaine was the girl. She was new at the time; hadn't danced or been in a musical. So we had to try to design something for her. She was a dramatic actress and had won an award for something. Lovely girl. But she said to me years later, 'You know that picture I did with you? It set my career back four years.' Bless her heart. It was a tough thing for her to do, you know.

Hastily RKO repaired what damage it could by reuniting the partnership for a new Berlin musical, *Carefree* (1938). Box-office response was good but not good enough to suggest that Astaire and Rogers could hold their position alongside Gable and Shirley Temple as the industry's safest financial investments. *The Story of Vernon and Irene Castle* (1939) was a mere Fred-and-Ginger afterthought, hardly regarded as part of the sequence today, not particularly because of its shortcomings but because, being the biography of a real-life team from the past, it was endowed with no original music. In any case, Astaire, aware that he had achieved so much that to achieve any more might prove impossible, was already flirting with the idea of retirement. Fortunately the idea is best represented in his professional life as a mirage which kept receding each time he approached it, but, in view of the amount of

Carefree (1938): an on-lot line-up during filming (*top*) includes director Mark Sandrich, Ginger, Ralph Bellamy, and Luella Gear; two of the dance sequences – 'Change Partners' (*above*) for which Fred hypnotizes Ginger and 'The Yam' (*opposite, above*); and shooting the stunning golf dance (*opposite, below*) – it took ten days of eight-hour sessions to rehearse, 2½ days to film.

The Castles Step Out

The period biopic *The Story of Vernon and Irene Castle*, a curiously uncharacteristic end to the Astaire-Rogers Thirties sequence: auditioning for comic Lew Fields (played by himself) to 'Waiting for the Robert E. Lee' (*opposite*); and three Castle Specials – the Walk (*above*), the Tango (*top*), and the Polka (*right*).

work which still lay before him, it is somehow
slightly shocking that at so early a stage–he was
still only in his late thirties–he should have
considered seriously the idea of never working
again.

Or at least, not as a dancer. The musician in
him never rested. Thirty years after *Carefree* he
was still as far from real thoughts of retirement
as ever:

Oh, I played the piano. I took lessons when I
was a kid. I can really play, but I play kind of
careless. I play by ear a lot. Well, I play all
right. I have a piano in my bedroom and
sometimes I get up at night and a tune comes to
me and I try to play it. Sometimes I'm too
tired to play it so I forget it next morning. I
don't know.

Astaire has defined himself as a proud
member of the composers' trade union, The
American Society of Composers, Authors and
Publishers, but adds that he is 'the dregs of their
list'. This is scandalously untrue, as his most
famous collaborator, Johnny Mercer, says:

Because he liked to write songs in his spare
time we got to be friendly. I made a record
with Ginger and I got talking with Fred and
he told me he had this song he wanted to
write called 'I'm Building Up to an Awful
Let-Down'. So he gave me the front eight
bars and I went home and added to it.

'I'm Building Up to an Awful Let-Down'
actually entered the Hit Parade in 1935, and
although the other Astaire songs, especially
'Hello Baby' and 'Just Like Taking Candy
From a Baby', have been disappointments so
far as commercial success goes, they all confirm
Astaire's authenticity as a minor practitioner of
the arts of Berlin, Gershwin and company. The
ASCAP Biographical Dictionary for 1966 lists
eight published Astaire compositions, and,
although it would be absurd to deny that with
the end of the partnership with Ginger a phase
of Astaire's life had finished, there is at least one
sense in which his career was to proceed in an
unbroken sequence, the sense of maintaining
his status as the prime interpreter of the work of
America's major composers.

CHANGE PARTNERS
and Dance...

HAYWORTH, CHARISSE AND OTHERS

BY 1940 in Hollywood the balance of musical power had shifted for the third and last time. With the advent of the Talkies, Warner Brothers had taken a long lead; by 1935 RKO – with Astaire – had passed them; but by the end of the decade MGM, with its limitless resources, was ready to dominate the screen musical. It was inevitable that Louis B. Mayer should eventually cast covetous eyes on Astaire, who moved over to MGM in 1939 to begin work on a one-off, *Broadway Melody of 1940*: it wouldn't be until 1945 that MGM producer Arthur Freed put him under contract. His partner was one of the great tap-dancers of the age, Eleanor Powell, and the music was by Cole Porter. Because from now on there was no female partner who made more than two successive pictures with Astaire, an account of his career becomes a somewhat disjointed cavalcade punctuated by more of those amazing moments where for a split second popular art seems to pause and contemplate itself through Astaire's dancing and singing. In *Broadway Melody* with 'I Concentrate on You', in *You Were Never Lovelier* with 'Dearly Beloved', in *The Sky's the Limit* with 'One for My Baby', the list might be extended indefinitely; an album issued years later in which Fred sings only those songs closely associated with him included more than forty standard items.

Retirement continued to be something talked about, considered, planned for, but never quite accepted. During the war Astaire went to Europe to entertain the troops, and when he returned home, two more scripts were awaiting him, one for *Yolanda and the Thief* (1945), the other for *The Ziegfeld Follies* (1946). The latter is one of the most famous of all Astaire's films, an item which would justify its selection for inclusion in one of those time-proof capsules which self-conscious epochs often bury deep in the ground for the delectation of future civilisations. The film preserves the most celebrated dance duet in cinema history, the one between Astaire and his successor as Hollywood's most innovative dancer, Gene Kelly. The song featured was one which belonged deep in Fred's Broadway past, so perhaps it is not surprising that it appealed more to Fred than to Kelly, who remembers the incident in slightly ambivalent terms:

The thing I remember most plainly about 'The Babbit and the Bromide' was the rehearsals. Of course Fred was the senior partner and if I felt there was any conflict or any doubt about any step I would certainly defer to him, but he made it so there wasn't

right
In *Broadway Melody of 1940* Fred was half a dancing team, the other half being George Murphy. The plot revolved round a mix-up over their names.

opposite
The screen's top male and female tap-dancers, Fred Astaire and Eleanor Powell, were paired only once, in *Broadway Melody of 1940*. The picture shows them rehearsing.

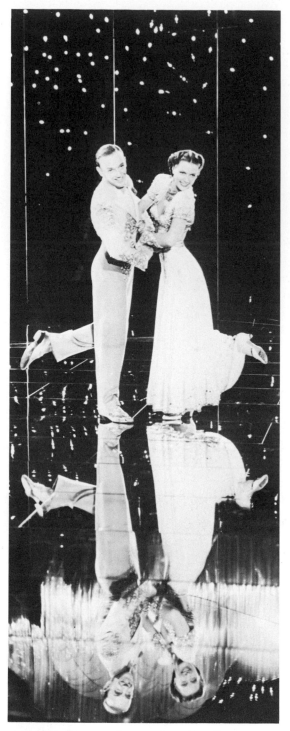

any. Wasn't a gentler or nicer man I ever
worked with. That isn't to say Fred isn't a
very tough worker. He can be as hard as nails,
and I've seen him be that way, but he's only
that way because he wants his dances as well
as can be. Fred felt good about the number
because he had done it before, in a show
together with his sister Adele.

Harry Warren, a three-time Academy
award-winning composer who had been responsible for most of the true elegance to be
found in the old Busby Berkeley pictures, now
found himself working with Astaire for the
first time:

It was a scary challenge. I always had this
feeling I wouldn't please him, and I wanted to
please him. He was always such a gentleman.
You wouldn't know if you pleased him or
not. He always talked the same way. He'd
say, 'It's very nice. I like it.' He was a quiet
kind of guy to talk to. He was that way all the
time. I don't think he ever said one word
about anything. If he didn't like something, he
would never come out with it.

Warren is being excessively modest; Astaire
accepted his work because he deeply admired
it, and justifiably so; for *The Ziegfeld Follies*
Warren presented Fred with 'This Heart of
Mine'.

The year was 1946, and by now Fred seemed
resolved on making no more films. As if to
tempt him further into retirement, the fates
conspired to let him achieve one of his most
deeply cherished ambitions, to own a
thoroughbred racehorse capable of winning
classic races. The horse's name was Triplicate,
and, in the period when Triplicate was bringing home winning purses amounting to a
quarter of a million dollars, Astaire actually
was living the life of a man who has finally put
his profession aside. The circumstances in
which he was cajoled into a comeback remain
obscure. According to Bing Crosby, 'I suppose
somebody in the studio thought it would be a
good idea to team us up.' But if Joan Caulfield
is to be believed, Crosby is being disingenuous.
Miss Caulfield recalls:

I first met Astaire on the set of *Blue Skies*
]1946] a picture with Crosby and Paul Draper
the dancer. We had had a week of production
and scenes weren't flowing, and that is
putting it mildly. Draper had a speech
difficulty. So one afternoon Bing said, 'I think
that'll be about it.' He excused himself, went
to the Front Office, and the next thing I
know, Fred Astaire was going to be on the set
on Monday morning. And he was.

After *Blue Skies* Astaire again attempted
retirement, and again circumstances conspired
to frustrate him. He has described how one day
in 1948 he was at home playing a recording by
Lionel Hampton of 'Jack the Bellboy' and
knocking himself out when the thought
suddenly occurred to him that he 'might as
well be doing this someplace where it counts'.
There was, however, nowhere to do it–at
which point there came another cry for help,
this time from Kelly:

I had worked for several weeks on *Easter Parade*; we were ready to shoot the film, and I was playing games in my backyard, and I broke my ankle. A couple of us went after the ball and my ankle cracked. The producer then started crying, literally. He started crying over the phone. He had a great aptitude for this. It was one of his greatest talents. I've never found out the others. So I said, 'Why not get Astaire?' Then Fred called me and he said, 'Look here, I don't want to do this. Why don't you wait and then do it?' The perfect gentleman. Whatever blessing I was empowered to give him, I gave.

Easter Parade (1948), co-starring Judy Garland, is often thought of today as the one featuring 'A Couple of Swells', or perhaps as the one in which Astaire, forging an astonishing alliance between technology and choreography, slows down the movement of the film in 'Steppin' Out with My Baby', achieving a synthesis of rhythmic half-time and visual slow-motion. The production was so successful that a second Garland–Astaire film was immediately scheduled for the following year, and at this juncture in Astaire's career, with events about to take an unpredictable and even melodramatic turn, it is revealing to see how what appear to be bold strokes of studio policy are usually blind gambles dictated by events.

Astaire had noticed during the making of *Easter Parade* that Judy Garland was working under acute difficulties caused by illness and vagaries of temperament; he doubted if she would prove strong enough to complete another major film so soon afterwards. This raised the age-old question of a new partner. But who? Ever since Fred's departure to MGM in 1940, the succession had been a disputed affair, with actress after actress flung into the breach to achieve sporadic and not always artistically satisfying results. In 1941–2 he had teamed up with the daughter of old vaudeville contemporaries, the Cansinos; at the age of twelve Adele had developed a crush on Mr

opposite
Fred and Betty Hutton in the 'Oh Them Dudes' routine from *Let's Dance*, one of the raucous numbers more suited to Hutton's style and delivery in this notable misalliance of talents. Astaire nonetheless enjoyed working with the lady, though he complained '. . . if you don't watch yourself you feel you're standing still and letting her do all the work.'

below
Rita Hayworth, only 3½ inches shorter than Fred, could not wear very high heels for their dancing in *You'll Never Get Rich* (1941).

Cansino, who was then nineteen and married; Fred remembered Cansino as 'a terrific Spanish dancer'; his daughter, whose professional name was Rita Hayworth, was also terrific in her own way, and has since been nominated by many people as the partner Fred liked the best, although Fred himself has maintained a life-long diplomatic silence on the subject. Among the other candidates had been Eleanor Powell, Paulette Goddard, Marjorie Reynolds, Joan Leslie and Olga San Juan; probably the most unusual had been Lucille Bremer, whom Vincente Minnelli described as 'a marvellous dancer, but rather cold. The warmth didn't come through. A marvellous girl to know but I don't think she ever really wanted to be a movie star. She got out of it as quickly as she could.'

Which left MGM with a problem. Who solved it has never been altogether clear. Adolph Green, who was collaborating with Betty Comden on the script, says, 'We were severely disappointed when we heard Judy wasn't going to make it. So we all huddled together and suddenly came up with—let's get those kids together again, Fred and Ginger.' Ginger later explained that she had been telephoned by the studio and then sent a script. She liked it and did it: 'It was as simple as that.'

In fact it was the least simple thing in the world. For one thing the reunion created so powerful an undertow of nostalgia that it proved almost too much for some people. The director Chuck Walters was quite overcome:

I'll never forget that day. Fred was rehearsing 'Shoes With Wings On'. Ginger Rogers came down the aisle, up on stage, and when they embraced I started to cry, because of the reunion and the years of adoration and worship. I just broke down. I couldn't believe I would be directing Astaire and Rogers.

Fred woos the beautiful 22-year-old Rita Hayworth in his irresistible way – by singing and dancing – in *You'll Never Get Rich*. Cole Porter based this haunting song on a tune written for an earlier Broadway musical 'Anything Goes'.

So Near and Yet So Far

Fred and family. Making sure young Freddy Astaire Jr starts life on the right foot (*opposite*). Freddy started dancing when two years old, and dad was quoted as saying, 'He rattles around a bit whenever he hears music'. Fred and wife Phyllis (*left*), and over in Britain for the Goodwood races in 1956, Fred relaxes with daughter Ava in the grounds of his Bognor Regis hotel (*below left*).

Fred and Rita Hayworth danced again in *You Were Never Lovelier* (1942). The pair in the number 'Shorty George' – to paraphrase the lyric 'beating their feet until their feet is beat'.

Mr Walters, however, very soon dried his tears when he realised that not everyone involved felt quite so ecstatic as he did. 'It was a thrill, but quite a shock to find that Mr Astaire is not too keen about Miss Rogers', to which Hermes Pan added, 'I don't think Fred was thrilled about it, because there again I think he felt it might be a step backwards, trying to recapture something that had happened before.' In the event *The Barkleys of Broadway* (1949) was a moderate success, notable for the brilliant solo Astaire dance 'Shoes with Wings On'.

It is, however, a picture worthy of examination for reasons not often used in assessing musical comedies. Comden and Green had injected into the plot certain overtones of reality too obvious to miss. In the story, Fred and Ginger are a husband-and-wife team who are successful on stage but who fight incessantly once they are off it. Arlene Croce dismisses the script as 'faintly horrible', and says that both the musicals which Comden and Green wrote for Astaire were 'slick and somewhat mordant variations on his career'.

The stricture is perhaps justified, but cannot alter the fact that, in attempting what was, to an extent, a roman à clef, Comden and Green were endowing the ordinary, commercial musical comedy with psychological implications not normally found or indeed looked for. The crowning irony of the *Barkleys of Broadway* episode is that in March 1950 Astaire was presented with a special Academy Award for his contribution to musicals. The award was handed to him by Ginger Rogers.

Astaire's next picture was one he later regarded with great warmth and affection, although it is likely that this was less to do with the merits of the film, which were not always easy to discern, than with its subject matter. In playing the role of Bert Kalmar in *Three Little Words* (1950), Astaire was becoming, at least for a moment, the successful songwriter he had always dreamed of being. Hermes Pan remembers the picture as one of the few in which Astaire 'could really dance instead of being limited by the girl', in this case Vera-Ellen.

On the theme of Astaire's virtuosity being

hobbled by unsuitable partnerships, Pan says of the next picture, *Let's Dance* (also 1950), co-starring Betty Hutton, 'A case of very bad casting. I must be honest. I don't think Fred should have been subjected to a partner who would limit him.' But the problem persisted. For the next Astaire picture, *Royal Wedding* (1951), June Allyson was selected to co-star but became pregnant; Judy Garland agreed to deputise but fell ill again; the third and final choice was Jane Powell. *Royal Wedding* was yet another poor film redeemed by Astaire's amazing technical as well as terpsichorean resource; in 'You're All The World To Me' he performs his apparently gravity-defying dance all over the ceiling and walls. *The Belle of New York* (1952), which followed *Royal Wedding*, again featured Vera-Ellen. Chuck Walters has suggested there was no 'chemistry' between leading man and leading lady, and that the whole production was 'a bit of a mish-mush'. Despite that, Astaire strove as usual to bring grace to the product, even though Walters could see that all was not well:

Fred was never happy with it. I'd be amazed at the lightness, the gaiety in a scene, and you'd say, 'Cut'; the face drops, the shoulders drop and he says, 'Oh, it's terrible. I can't stand it. I hate it.' It was a waste of time trying to convince him it was fine.

At this stage, with a long succession of indifferent Astaire movies saved from catastrophe only by Fred's own performances, there comes the film which may well qualify as the most fascinating in fifty years of the Hollywood musical. This is not simply because it is an outstanding film, although in many ways it is indeed outstanding, but because, in concocting their script for *The Band Wagon* (1953), Comden and Green were indulging in the unorthodoxy of writing a fictitious screenplay for a much-loved performer which was about the performer in real life. There had been a few wisps of half-truth in the assumptions behind *The Barkleys of Broadway*, but it is with *The Band Wagon* that the screen musical achieves a degree of self-examination.

Fred auditions all round the room and even on the desk for hotel owner Adolphe Menjou, who is not too happy about Fred's feelings for his daughter (Rita Hayworth) in *You Were Never Lovelier*.

You Were Never Lovelier

When Fred is moved to say 'You were never lovelier' to Rita Hayworth, the words provide not only the title of the film, but also prompt the orchestra to begin the melody which allows Fred and Rita to glide into one of those romantic dances which the audience have come in to see.

In *Ziegfeld Follies* (1946), a tribute to Florenz Ziegfeld, Fred danced for the first time with Gene Kelly. Both age throughout the dance 'The Babbitt and the Bromide', and in this scene they meet as elderly gentlemen with beards in heaven, their athleticism apparently unimpaired.

If *Singin' in the Rain* parodies the Talkies, *The Band Wagon* is the apotheosis of showbiz itself, the nearest thing to a roman à clef to which the genre has ever aspired. With a certain sly and ruthless cunning, those responsible for the work fashioned a picture which may be explored simultaneously on several different levels, for which reason it has become over the years a labyrinth of allusion to be explored lovingly by connoisseurs. So far as general audiences were concerned, it was just another item in the long line of backstage musicals. But for those versed in the traditions of the genre, *The Band Wagon* is easily the most revealing musical picture ever made.

The husband-and-wife team of Comden and Green wrote a screenplay about a husband-and-wife team writing a stage show for a fading movie star returning to Broadway, knowing even as they wrote it that the part would be played by a middle-aged movie star whose reputation had originally been made on Broadway:

The dream ballet from *Yolanda and the Thief* (1945), a 16-minute sequence in which Fred dreams he meets Yolanda (Lucille Bremer) and falls in love with her as her veils ensnare him in a clinging dance – he wakes entangled in the sheets of his bed.

We took a very simple idea, to try to bring to a theatre story a lot of what we knew from having written for theatre and try to do it sort of realistically. A backstage musical, if you like.

In the story, the musical they write falls into the hands of a musical whizz-kid with ideas about Culture; Comden and Green knew their scenario was to be directed by Vincente Minnelli. In the story, the show founders under its own weight, and after a catastrophic out-of-town tryout, there is the obligatory scene where the male half of the writing team, played by Oscar Levant, says, 'Gosh, with all this talent around, why can't us kids get together and put on our own show?' It is the standard Rooney–Cagney speech for the occasion, except that this time, twenty years after the event, Levant stops in mid-flow, carefully underplaying the parodic nature of the moment; the joke is there to be picked up by those who care to. But there is another, for in creating the married writing-team, Comden and Green were planting themselves firmly inside their own story, transmuting themselves into fictitious entities, as in the scene where the couple comprise a forlorn welcoming committee at Grand Central Station for the ageing hoofer Tony Hunter; in real life Green had

The 'Heat Wave' number from *Blue Skies* (1946) tested Fred's acrobatic ability to the full, as he had to fall from a bridge during the dance. This still shows him in his more usual smooth style with Olga San Juan in his arms.

Irving Berlin's *Blue Skies* included a number called 'A Couple of Song and Dance Men', and what better couple could there be than Fred and Bing Crosby.

once played this scene when meeting Comden.

But at its deepest level *The Band Wagon* is about Astaire; the circumstances of his career so dominate the plot that it is true to say – and Comden and Green have said it – that had Astaire not experienced that career there would be no film at all. The plot concerns Tony Hunter, a washed-up song-and-dance man who returns from Hollywood to Broadway and is paired off with the pride of the ballet, played by Cyd Charisse. But when the two first meet, Hunter keeps peering up at the crown of her head, trying to work out if she is too tall for him: Eleanor Powell has described how, in 1939 when Louis B. Mayer interviewed her as a possible new partner for Fred in *Broadway Melody of 1940*, she had been in the room several minutes before Astaire, who had

been hiding behind the door measuring her up, revealed himself. Cyd Charisse experienced the identical scrutiny in the run-up to *The Band Wagon*; Fred has defined her as 'bigger than Ginger but not too big'. The tensions in Comden and Green's plot are generated by the mutual mistrust of the hoofer and the ballerina; throughout his career Astaire displayed an ambivalence if not towards his partners, then to the implications of partnership. Working in harness seems to have presented him with certain psychological difficulties, and by the time of *The Band Wagon* he had been obliged to suffer one or two leading ladies of stupefying ineptitude.

The parallels run deeper. In the scene where Levant makes his 'kids' speech, Hunter cheers up the assembled cast by singing a song called 'I

Love Louisa', which Astaire had introduced in the 1931 Broadway revue also called 'The Band Wagon'. When he first arrives back in New York, Hunter is appalled by the changes since his day. Looking around, he asks, 'Where's the New Amsterdam? I had one of my biggest hits there.' The New Amsterdam was where Fred and Adele had opened in 'The Band Wagon', their last show together. When Hunter first sees the ballerina who is to be his new partner, she is dancing 'Giselle', but the music is 'Beggar's Waltz' by Arthur Schwartz, who composed all 'The Band Wagon' music.

Throughout the action there is this sense of being shuttled from one plane of reality to another, particularly in the scene at the end where Hunter, having triumphed at last, is distressed that nobody has dropped by to his dressing-room. 'What's the matter?' he asks. 'Don't people come backstage any more?' Is this Hunter speaking, or Astaire, who left the live theatre in 1934 never to return? It was by planting their story in the rich subsoil of the real past that Comden and Green gave *The Band Wagon* its surprising emotional impact. As we familiarise ourselves with the facts of Astaire's life, layer after layer of the onion of *The Band Wagon*'s contrivance is peeled away to reveal – what?

Essentially *The Band Wagon* is a valedictory. Astaire had been flirting with retirement for years. But the film is a last gesture in a more significant way. By 1953 the Hollywood musical had been living off its capital for a long time. In the euphoria of Kelly's two master-strokes, *Singin' in the Rain* and *An American in*

Fred performs a zany dance in a toy-store in *Easter Parade*. He impresses nine-year-old Jimmy Bates by using drums of various sizes as props. In the still at the bottom, he is not only tapping out the rhythm with his feet and drum sticks, but adding the drum beats by hitting the big drum behind him with his head.

Drum Crazy

Paris, it went unremarked that neither of those two productions had contained so much as a bar of original music. Few people at the time noticed the significance of this, but one who did was Kelly, who says that by the time he arrived in Hollywood in 1942 he felt he was ten years too late for the creative composers, who had by then either died or written themselves out. Even as *The Band Wagon* triumphed, television was moving in to destroy that studio system without which Arthur Freed's musical repertory company at MGM could never have hoped to survive. *The Band Wagon* therefore remains something special in its genre. To claim its libretto as a victory for realism may seem bizarre, but there is a sense in which the claim is justified. What Astaire and company so brilliantly succeeded in doing was to preserve on celluloid the reality of a fantasy, the fantasy of musical comedy.

There is one moment in *The Band Wagon* when the exhilaration of Astaire's dancing is inspired by the very forces of change and

decline which had made such a performance obsolescent. The disillusioned Hunter goes in search of the New Amsterdam, only to find that the entire area has sunk into squalor. Minnelli describes the tensions which motivate the dance:

He was bewailing the fact that 52nd Street was so run down, and that the theatre where he'd played with great stars was given over to crummy movies, souvenir shops, flea circuses and so on. And then he arrives in this penny arcade, doing a number there.

The sequence is yet another which belongs in that anthology of the dance to which Astaire has contributed so prolifically. By a fortunate coincidence, its filming was witnessed by someone whose professional experience was profound enough for him to sense the skill and dedication it demanded, but whose detachment from the musical form clarified his vision of the event. Concurrently with *The Band*

opposite
Ginger Rogers teamed up with Fred again in *The Barkleys of Broadway* (1949). Playing a husband-and-wife song and dance team, they presented many of their dances as parts of stage shows within the film's story, including 'My One and Only Highland Fling', a broad Scottish number.

above
Ginger wants to leave musicals for drama in *The Barkleys of Broadway*, strangely recalling her real-life desire to change the direction of her career. Her choice of understudy fell on Gale Robbins.

Shoes with Wings On

The shoe-mender sketch
from *The Barkleys of
Broadway*: a pair of white
shoes dance by themselves,
Fred puts them on, dances,

other pairs join in – and
Fred, having failed with a
broom, resorts to pistols to
bring the whole crazy whirl
to an end.

Wagon MGM was filming its prestigious version of 'Julius Caesar', in which Sir John Gielgud played Cassius:

They said Fred Astaire was filming on a set nearby so would I like to meet him? I rushed over and he was doing a shoeshine number. They said he had sweated his way through four grey flannel suits that morning doing the number over and over again. I was staggered, because I had never seen a musical film being made, at the way he could begin in the middle of a dance. He was having a shoeshine on a sort of pier, and he jumped over the bootblack's back and rushed into a shooting gallery and he made havoc there, and there were all sorts of gags. Of course the soundtrack had already been recorded and his singing was coming through the loudspeaker and he had to mime the words and I was amazed that he could begin halfway through

the shot. All timed to perfection without losing a beat of music or appearing to be put out by the fact that he wasn't really singing at all. The skill was amazing. I was amazed at his painstaking thoroughness and extraordinary accuracy.

Further aspects of reality obtruded into the make-believe world of Tony Hunter, who is shown as a hoofer distinctly apprehensive of teaming up with a legitimate ballet dancer. The real-life Astaire has said, 'I didn't like ballet too much. Too cut and dried. That wasn't my racket; I just couldn't do it and didn't want to do it, so I went into the more popular type–as you might say the more remunerative type–of entertainment. I'm not knocking ballet. I think it's terrific for those who do it, but I didn't want to. I wanted to do something else.'

By a tragic mischance there was one other aspect of *The Band Wagon* which accidentally

Three Little Words (1950) was the Hollywood version of the lives of songwriters Harry Ruby (Red Skelton) and Bert Kalmar (Fred Astaire). Vera-Ellen is Mrs Kalmar in this 'Suppose we try it like this' scene.

The 'Where Did You Get That Girl?' number from *Three Little Words*. Mr and Mrs Bert Kalmar dance at the Palace Theatre in 1919.

impinged on reality, the moment when Astaire steps off the train at Grand Central, realises that the press has no interest in him, and saunters down the platform singing a song called 'By Myself', written by Schwartz and Dietz fifteen years before for one of the featured players in the film, Jack Buchanan. The song is a masterly exposition of the fatalistic shrug of the shoulders and the gesture of brave defiance in the face of loneliness, and has since been read by over-zealous interpreters as a reflection of Astaire's private anguish at the time. That such interpretations are founded on an imperception of the distinction between life as it is lived and performance as it is achieved by the application of intense technical expertise is beside the point; people continue to draw these bogus parallels because it assuages their hunger for melodrama, just as thousands of mourners for Judy Garland persist in seeing 'The Man Who Got Away' as a statement of the singer's personal crisis.

above
In *Let's Dance* (1950) Fred performs a 'Piano Dance' which includes snatches of 'Tiger Rag', allowing him to dance all over the piano while pianist Tommy Chambers remains unruffled.

opposite
Fred falls in love with Sarah Churchill in *Royal Wedding* (1951). Propping up her picture in his hotel room, he discovers its presence can inspire him to dance literally all round the room. 'You're All the World to Me' was performed with the furniture and fittings fixed and the room revolving.

You're All the World to Me

left
Fred Astaire, Nanette Fabray and Jack Buchanan in 'The Triplets' number from *The Band Wagon* (1953).

below left
Two very elegant song-and-dance men, Jack Buchanan and Astaire do the old soft shoe to 'I Guess I'll Have to Change My Plan' from *The Band Wagon.*

below
Same film, different mood. Le Roy Daniels gives Fred 'A Shine on Your Shoes'.

opposite
Publicity still for *The Belle of New York* (1952). Vera-Ellen tells Fred love makes you 'walk on air', and, strange to relate, up in the air they go.

The Band Wagon has the old plot about getting a terrible show faced with major disasters onto the road and transformed into a smash-hit by the last reel. 'The Girl Hunt', danced by Astaire and Cyd Charisse, is the show-stopper. As a private eye pursuing a killer, Fred encounters in various guises Cyd Charisse and an assortment of hoods.

The Girl Hunt

The retrospective significance of Astaire's wonderfully charming performance of 'By Myself' at the start of *The Band Wagon* is that by the time he performed it he must have been aware that Phyllis was gravely ill and might not survive. Because the production of *The Band Wagon* is the only instance in all Astaire's career of a fellow-professional complaining of his manner, his personal grief does have some relevance. Nanette Fabray, who portrays the part of the scriptwriting wife in the picture, has given labyrinthine examples of Astaire's abruptness and indifference to her problems during the shooting of various sequences. She later said, 'I had been inquiring what was wrong, why everyone was so strange on the set, and it had something to do with his wife's illness. He was aloof, cold, remote. He would come in and do his work and just disappear.' In the light of this observation, Gielgud's tribute becomes more impressive than ever.

In the spring of 1954 Phyllis underwent a major operation, recovered against all odds, suffered a relapse in the summer, and died on 13 September, 1954. Astaire is such a private man, who cherished his married life so zealously, who loved his wife so deeply, that even twenty-five years later, it seems like an intrusion for a perfect stranger to discuss the events of 1954. Perhaps the most tactful way of commenting on them is to quote two of his closest friends, Hermes Pan and David Niven.

Pan remembers, 'He took it very bad. No, not bad, that's the wrong word. But it did affect him greatly. I think it was a loss he will never recover from. I've never seen a marriage as completely happy as theirs. So even today he will think, "Oh, wouldn't it be wonderful if Phyllis could share this or that", so I think that when she died a part of his life was sort of ended.' Niven has told in his autobiography of a curious reaction by Astaire to his own grief; the story was later corroborated by Astaire:

It was about six months after I lost Phyllis. I just got this idea. There were some blue mail boxes in the neighbourhood and I thought, 'Gee, that's all I have to do. There was a red top and a blue bottom to the mail box, and all I have to do is wrap some yellow round the middle, and that's my racing colours, red cap, yellow sash and blue blouse.' So I set out on this little job. If I'd been caught, I don't know what they would have done to me, messing around with mail boxes. It was so silly. But I was in a very difficult frame of mind in those days and felt so terrible about what had

happened. The loss was a terrific thing to try to accept—the children were wonderful all through this thing, of course—so all of a sudden I got this idea, and the mail boxes stayed that way for about a week. I suppose nobody saw me do it. I was very sneaky about the whole thing. It was just a kind of mood thing to get myself back to earth again.

Of course Astaire had no appetite left for work. He was, however, committed to a new production of that hoary fable, *Daddy Long Legs* (1955), in which a young girl falls for a man old enough to be her father. Understandably he doubted his ability to continue with his work.

Adele
One night Fred came to me and said, 'You know, I don't think I can go on with this film, I just don't feel I can do it. My heart isn't here.' This very nice producer said, 'You're letting the whole company down. You can't do that. It's not going to help matters', and he talked him into it and Fred went ahead with it. If you see that picture today, you would never know he had sadness of any kind.

The Astaire image as it will be best remembered. A publicity still from 1940 (*opposite*) and a dance from 1950 (*right*) both show Fred in immaculate formal attire, groomed to the last hair on his head and elegantly button-holed, ready to descend on the town and flutter the female hearts.

opposite
A pipe seems slightly out-of-character for Astaire, but he 'wore' one for 'History of the Beat', a drum-and-dance sequence from *Daddy Long Legs* (1955).

above left
Before she meets her anonymous sponsor, college girl Leslie Caron daydreams about him in *Daddy Long Legs*. Fred appears in her dream as millionaire and playboy, then finally as her guardian angel.

above right
In his pursuit of Audrey Hepburn in *Funny Face* (1957), Fred poses with fake beard as an Empatheticalist, a follower of a philosophical movement led by a Sartre-like figure with whom Hepburn is staying. The deception leads to this rousing message to the faithful, 'Clap Yo' Hands', with Kay Thompson.

below
In more tender mood Fred, as a fashion photographer, dances the title number from *Funny Face* with his new model, Audrey Hepburn, transformed from a dowdy bookshop assistant.

Astaire has said that in retrospect it seems
fortunate that he was involved in the making of
Daddy Long Legs:

That helped. It's a hard thing to accept it and
have to be as busy as I was. I was working
with Leslie Caron and the picture was good. I
loved the movie, and was glad to be able to
do it. There was a lot of work to do, so the
only thing was that there would be a reaction
later on.

The successor to *Daddy Long Legs* was a movie
version of 'Funny Face', in which Fred and
Adele had scored so many years before. The
director, Stanley Donen, has remarked that the
stage show had 'absolutely no relationship to
the film', which is an interesting example of the
extent to which even people inside the profession can fail to grasp the simple truth of the
musical-comedy form, which is that first in
order of precedence, before the plot, the script,
the cast, and, dare one say it, before even the
director, comes the music; in the 1957 Paramount version of *Funny Face*, the score

included the title song, 'He Loves and She
Loves', 'Let's Kiss and Make Up' and
'S'Wonderful' from the original production,
and the film stands in the Astaire canon as the
movie with the most effective and imaginative
use of colour photography.

Funny Face is also noteworthy in another
way; its soundtrack became available, which
was a heresy in the mid- to late- 1950s. The
process by which this came about is revealed in
passing by Kay Thompson, who had a featured
role in the picture:

There wasn't too much conversation with
Fred. The niceties and pleasantries of the day
didn't enter into it. He stuck to himself, or his
dressing room. On *Funny Face* he talked to
Norman Granz a lot; Granz was the owner of
Verve Records, the company that put out the
Funny Face album. I think if Norman had had
his way he would have had Fred record all his
dance routines. He was mad on the subject
and rightly so; Norman is a very tasty fellow.
And he did the album of *Funny Face* really
exquisitely.

opposite and above
Astaire at home: the golfing
shot taken in 1968, the other
some two years later.
Always a private man, he
did not alter with age and
semi-retirement. He was still
playing golf, and pool, still
following the horses.

The *Funny Face* album was by no means Granz's first involvement with Astaire; just before production began on *The Band Wagon*, he had proposed that Fred re-record forty of the songs most closely associated with him, not with the usual orchestral accompaniment, but with a small jazz group. The collection subsequently appeared as *The Fred Astaire Story*, and disclosed variations in interpretation which must have gratified Astaire in particular. Always enough of a musician to understand that the most perceptive interpreters of all are jazz musicians, he realised that in collaborating with players like Oscar Peterson, Ray Brown, Charlie Shavers and Flip Phillips he was setting his own vocal style in a more flattering frame than ever before. Some of the tempos were considerably slower than in early recordings, and the keys tended to be a tone lower here and there, but these later versions, far from being inferior to the originals, were in several instances far more subtle and sophisticated in the musical

sense. 'Isn't This a Lovely Day' is one example among many of how a more leisurely pace and the beautifully rounded playing of master-accompanists can cast a familiar voice in a new light. The forty tracks, which also included two extraordinary duets between Peterson at the piano and Astaire tap-dancing, have long since become collector's items.

The great dancing career had now almost run its course, and *Silk Stockings* (1957), the picture which followed *Funny Face*, was the last musical comedy in which Astaire was ever to star as hero. For that reason, it was perhaps unfortunate that, in spite of a favourable critical reaction, *Silk Stockings* was one of Cole Porter's least inspired scores, with only 'All of You' to qualify remotely as standard material; in fact, the movie score commended itself by using two vintage Porter songs, 'You'd Be So Nice to Come Home To' and 'I've Got You Under My Skin' as background themes. Astaire has said that after *Silk Stockings* he was

above
In his first non-musical film, *On The Beach* (1959), the 60-year-old Astaire was an alcoholic English scientist, who in a grim story about nuclear disaster nevertheless provided a little light relief by indulging his fancy for racing Ferraris.

opposite
With Petula Clark, playing daughter Sharon, in *Finian's Rainbow*. Among the other credits is Hermes Pan: dance director. This was the old firm's sixteenth job together.

Finian's Rainbow (1968) was a lavish film version of the successful stage musical. Fred was an Irish immigrant who steals a crock of gold from a leprechaun. Here he dances the 'Look to the Rainbow' sequence while Petula Clark sings the lyrics (*right*), co-stars alongside English leprechaun Tommy Steele (*below*), and toasts the day 'When the Idle Poor Become the Idle Rich' (*opposite*).

Fred rehearses with Barrie Chase. She had first appeared alongside him in *Silk Stockings*, but in the late Fifties and Sixties she was a welcome addition to many of his television shows, including 'An Evening with Fred Astaire' (1958), 'Astaire Time' (1960), 'Hollywood Palace' (1966), and 'The Fred Astaire Show' (1968).

offered several new musical scripts, and deduced from the fact that none of them appealed to him that his days in musical pictures were over.

He was very nearly right, but his career had yet to yield a few remarkable afterthoughts, like his prizewinning television spectaculars and his stark, markedly non-musical portrayal of an ageing playboy scientist in the nuclear melodrama, *On the Beach* (1959). At the age of sixty-eight, after a six-year absence from the movies, Astaire returned as Finian McLonergan in an indifferent Warner Brothers production of *Finian's Rainbow* (1968), in which his vocal delivery was embellished by the accent of a stage Irishman. The picture was of little consequence when measured against the TV shows, which, besides giving Astaire the opportunity to sing all his old favourites, provided him with the last outstanding dancing partner of his career, Barrie Chase.

Everyone concerned has testified to the outstanding qualities of Miss Chase and her benign effect on Astaire:

Pan
She was a marvellous dancer. Great quality, great movement. She was one of the three girls in *Silk Stockings*, and has always been an excellent dancer.

Much of the choreography on the TV spectaculars was done by Herbert Ross, who says of the Astaire–Chase partnership:

He just worshipped her. He thought she was the best partner he'd ever had and one of the best dancers in the world. He never tired of watching her dance, and indeed she was wonderful.
Adele
She vibrated him, as he'd say. Filled him full of vibes. I think that's what happened. She was so inspiring to him, and was such a beautiful dancer. And a little temperamental too, which he liked. So they got on beautifully together.

Astaire has said that she was one of the reasons that he did the TV shows in the first place:

At that point I was around sixty, and to have a very young girl working with you at sixty, well I didn't want to be up against somebody saying, 'My God, what's that old guy doing with that kid?' But she just had that sophisticated manner. You would never say,

'My goodness, why is that little girl with that old goat?' Well, I thought maybe I wasn't that old, but there's an age difference that bothers them in dance, you know. But Barrie was able to look right in whatever she did, and that's a good thing. It's hard to describe her. I don't know.

The Astaire career did not so much end as slowly fade away, in a diminuendo of non-musical roles in television and pictures, one of which, *The Towering Inferno* (1975), won an Oscar nomination. By the time he was seen watching his youthful self in the MGM compilation *That's Entertainment* (1974) and its sequel, *That's Entertainment Part 2* (1976), Astaire had become the symbol of his generation, the brilliant epitome of an age in popular art when quality was the final arbiter.

In the disaster movie *The Towering Inferno* (1975) passion blazes with the skyscraper as Fred, playing a confidence trickster, genuinely falls in love with his victim, Jennifer Jones, who inconsiderately dies in the inferno, serving Fred right.

right
That's Entertainment (1974) was a run-through of clips from MGM musical hits, and became a hit itself. Fred Astaire and Gene Kelly, the leading figures in screen dancing, were two of the co-presenters, as well as stars of many of the excerpts.

below right
The success of *That's Entertainment* led to a 'son of', with the inspired title *That's Entertainment Part 2* (1976). Astaire and Gene Kelly co-presented this compilation, and Fred joined Kelly in four new sequences as well as appearing in many of the old clips. Before the London premiere, the two dancers strolled in the Embankment Gardens with two of Fred's partners from the great days, Cyd Charisse and Leslie Caron.

opposite
Astaire's dancing has sometimes led to his singing skill being overlooked, but he has an easy and accomplished way with a lyric. He joined the Old Groaner on this United Artists record called simply – and who needs more – Bing Crosby and Fred Astaire.

THEY CAN'T TAKE THAT
Away From Me

THE GREATEST DANCER IN THE MOVIES

ASTAIRE'S uniqueness had long been apparent when the MGM retrospectives underlined the fact. People understood that there would never be anybody with whom to compare him, to duplicate the range of his achievement, least of all to replace him.

From the scattered testimony of contemporaries, from his own words, and from the written and filmed evidence, we can piece together at least a partial portrait. Astaire is a perfectionist, a virtuoso, a private man. Irving Berlin has defined him as 'a great perfectionist who works harder than anyone I know to get one step right'. Jerome Kern once administered a friendly rebuke to Hermes Pan for suggesting that a certain song wouldn't suit Astaire with the words, 'It's ridiculous to say that. Fred couldn't do anything bad.' Kelly calls him 'a very moderate, very conservative man. He doesn't drink, doesn't smoke. He's not a prude, he's just conservative.' The point is elaborated by Pan:

Fred is not what you'd call the most sociable person. He doesn't have a big circle of friends, and he hates to go to parties, big parties. It's considered the social feat of the year to get Astaire to come to a party. And sometimes he gets roped in and complains no end about it. If he goes to a party and some woman asks to dance with him, he is very kind and polite, but it kills him inside. He could die.

Apart from the fact that in all epochs an abhorrence of large parties has always been a sure sign of sensitivity and intelligence, Astaire's foibles mark him as a child of his generation, the last one to enjoy the comforting illusion that the world's possibilities are infinite. His exasperation at the needless complicating of daily existence with the bogus panaceas of modern science is perfectly caught in the following statement:

We never had any of these hangups. I don't know. Things were a lot different in my life. I never knew there was such a thing as a calorie. What is a calorie, anyway? I think it's a sad situation when people feel they're not being loved enough. I mean, if they're loved too much they don't like that either. I don't know. Fortunately, it never happened around me.

One of the best remembered images of Astaire: beating out the staccato rhythms of the 'Top Hat, White Tie and Tails' number from *Top Hat*.

In such moments Astaire's monumental normality actually seems almost abnormal. Emotionally fulfilled, first by a wise and doting mother, then by a loved and loving partner, finally by happy children, he has had no serious distractions from the business of his life, which has been to perform in public. Poor health might have been the last impediment, but no sign of it ever appeared:

I've been old a long time. I don't feel old, and you can't describe what being old is like until you get there. Fortunately I have no ailments and I think that's part of the battle.

His beloved daughter Ava quotes him as saying 'old is in the mind':

He says he knows he's old but it doesn't matter. He feels young so he doesn't care. He says he can't do the steps because it would be bad for his heart. But his voice still sounds young, you see.

Astaire's persistent youthfulness is vividly demonstrated by very recent exchanges with Astaire recalled for me by men I encountered in writing this book. The first described how Astaire, during a brief street-corner meeting in Beverly Hills, talked of the possibilities of someone recording his latest song; the second hustled me into his car and played me a cassette tape of Astaire singing at the piano; the composition was one of his own, and the performance was punctuated with those 'yeah's' and grunts of expression which are a sure sign that Astaire is totally absorbed.

Astaire's well-balanced psyche comes in part from his background, in part from the accident of temperament. He has always nominated his mother as one of the prime influences:

My mother was there when we were children. I know she was there later on. She's been terrific. In the early days she had to travel with us, and then when that stopped, around 1916, she stayed a great influence. She was an extraordinary woman anyway. A very gentle person. I don't know what you would say about your mother except that she was a smash mother. She knew what it was about, I'll tell you that.

In old age Astaire was always worried about leaving Beverly Hills for long in case his mother, who lived with the family, should fall ill. Well into her nineties she remained spry and

astute, and it was a sad irony that when she finally died, at the age of ninety-seven, her son should have been assisting at a premiere of *That's Entertainment Part 2* – in London, where he had been working nearly fifty years earlier when news arrived of the death of his father.

The burdens of greatness have been borne by Astaire only with much discomfort. Hollywood in the 1930s and 1940s was the last place for a man to live who craves privacy and the happy anonymity of family life:

I don't like publicity at all. I don't like the fundamental baloney that goes with great success. It's not easy to take. Publicity is not my racket. I don't like it. I don't seek it. I know you have to have a certain amount, to promote your movies, but this idea of having personal publicity is just simply not my cup of tea. And it certainly wasn't my wife's. She was no part of show business at all.

That last remark is no doubt a clue to the persistence with which Astaire, at the very peak of his career, pursued the mirage of retirement:

I had some plans. My wife and I were going to live in the country. I thought, 'I've done enough of this, I don't have to fool around with anything any more.' The reason for retiring is you get to the point where I'd say, 'All right, the next one is the last one, that's the end.' Then, the picture would be so good it led to more. I used to get letters from people saying I was setting a bad example to the youth of the nation by retiring. My God, I was old enough at the time not to be ashamed of retiring and I used to go to our ranch every weekend. She absolutely loved it. When I lost her I never went back there again. Without Phyllis it didn't mean anything.

There remains the question of Astaire's eventual place in the popular art of the century. All talk of assessment and greatness embarrasses him acutely, but, like the publicity which attended his films, it is unavoidable. Of his peers, Crosby has suggested that as a dancer Astaire is 'the greatest that ever lived. I don't see anybody to touch him. He had genius, plus hard work. He was indefatigable.' Gene Kelly has defined his significance more precisely:

He had an elegance that aligned itself with what I guess you'd call high society. In the 1930s, in the poor years in America it was very much needed. People said, 'Oh, look at those people dancing.' Visiting Venice or some place, in rooms that were all a-glitter with chrome and silver and white. The girls were all beautiful. No sweatshirts or jeans. It was a great escape for people. I do think the psychological position is underrated here. People wanted to see this sort of thing very much.

Of Astaire's two most perceptive critics, Arlene Croce and Pauline Kael, both of The New Yorker, it would be difficult to guess which has made the victim squirm the more with her eulogies. The fact that these eulogies were hard won and perfectly justified appears to be beside the point for Astaire, who resolutely refuses to be deified. Miss Croce has written that in the Fred-and-Ginger years 'dancing was transformed into a vehicle of serious emotion between a man and a woman.

It never happened in movies again.' Miss Kael crystallises the myth which Kelly struggled to describe in his talk of high society. She describes the whole series of Fred-and-Ginger dances as 'the most exquisite courtship rites the screen has ever known', and, judging wisely that Miss Croce's 'The Fred Astaire and Ginger Rogers Book' is the best that will ever be written on the subject, she sums up the dream as follows:

Astaire and Rogers were fortunate: they embodied the swing-music, white-telephone, streamline era before the Second World War, when frivolousness wasn't decadent and when adolescents dreamed that 'going out' was dressing up and becoming part of a beautiful world of top hats and silver lamé.

Both Miss Croce and Miss Kael have done what they could to express admiration for an astonishing career, but it seems likely that three other tributes have counted much more with the man on the receiving end. All his life Astaire has remained a student of, and a minor practitioner in, the art of popular songwriting. His feelings about the writers who provided his best material approach reverence. It is therefore probable that if Astaire can be convinced at all about his chances of immortality, then he believes they lie in the accolades bestowed upon him by the kind of men whose friendship and approval he has valued most highly of all.

In a 1934 stage musical called 'Anything Goes', Cole Porter wrote into the catalogue which comprises the lyric of 'You're the Top' the following lines:

> You're the nimble tread of the feet
>   of Fred Astaire,
> You're an O'Neill drama,
> You're Whistler's mama,
> You're Camembert.

Two years later Lorenz Hart, working in partnership with Richard Rodgers on a Broadway show called 'On Your Toes', wrote a set of words for the title song which, like Porter's 'You're the Top', dealt exclusively in superlatives:

> They climb the clouds
> to come through with
> airmail.
> The dancing crowds
> look up to some rare male
> like that Astaire male.

Four years later, in 'Pal Joey', Hart did it again, opening a lyric introduced on Broadway by Gene Kelly:

> Fred Astaire once worked so hard
>   he often lost his breath,
> and now he taps all other chaps to
>   death.

Yet another lyric-writing worshipper of Astaire is Alan Jay Lerner, who recounts the following revealing anecdote:

One evening in the dark grey hours of dusk, I was walking across the deserted MGM lot when a small, weary figure with a towel around his neck suddenly appeared out of one of the giant cube sound stages. It was Fred. He came over to me, threw a heavy arm around my shoulder and said, 'Oh, Alan, why doesn't someone tell me I can't dance?' The tormented illogic of his question made any answer insipid, and all I could do was walk with him in silence. Why doesn't someone tell Fred Astaire he cannot dance? Because no one would ever ask that question but Fred Astaire. Which is why he is Fred Astaire.

As to that, let the last word be with Fred Astaire himself:

I feel I just worked very hard to do something, and sometimes I liked what I did and sometimes I didn't like what I did. I've never been completely satisfied. Maybe when I see things I did, I like them better than I did at the time. But when you're on the spot you say, 'My, is this good enough?'

And then, with the twinkle in the eye, the line which might almost have come from Jerry Travers, or Bake Baker, or Lucky Garnett, or Pete Peters, or any of the other dancing, singing heroes that Astaire portrayed – except that the words are his:

What I'm most proud of is the fact that I made a buck. That's one thing that pleases me.

A true gentleman to the end, he tactfully omits to say that it has pleased everyone else too.

APPENDICES

STAGE CAREER

A record of Fred and Adele Astaire's Broadway and London musicals. Adele partnered him in all but the two productions of *Gay Divorce*. No attempt is made to distinguish those numbers Fred performed alone or with members of the cast other than, or as well as, Adele.

OVER THE TOP
Opened 28 November, 1917, at the 44th Street Theatre: 78 performances

Produced by Messrs Shubert. Directed by Joseph Herbert. Music directed by Frank Tours. Lyrics by Charles J. Manning and Matthew Woodward. Music by Sigmund Romberg and Herman Timberg. Sketches by Philip Bartholomae and Harold Atteridge. Dance director: Allan K. Foster. Settings: P. Dodd Ackerman.

WITH Justine Johnstone, Mary Eaton, T. Roy Barnes (succeeded by Ed Wynn), Craig Campbell, Ted Lorraine, Joe Laurie, Vivian and Dagmar Oakland, and Betty Pierce.
THEIR MUSICAL NUMBERS: 'Frocks and Frills', 'Where Is the Language to Tell?', and 'Justine Johnstone Rag'.

For Goodness Sake

THE PASSING SHOW OF 1918
Opened 25 July, 1918, at the Winter Garden, Broadway: 125 performances

Produced by Messrs Shubert. Directed by J. C. Huffman. Music directed by Charles Previn. Lyrics and sketches by Harold Atteridge. Music by Sigmund Romberg and Jean Schwartz. Dance director: Jack Mason. Settings: Watson Barratt.

WITH Frank Fay, Willie and Eugene Howard, Charles Ruggles, George Hassell, Sam White, Lou Clayton, Nita Naldi, Dave Dreyer, Jessie Reed, Nell Carrington, Isabel Lowe, Virginia Fox Brooks, Arthur Albro, Dorsha, Edith Pierce, Aileen Rooney, Emily Miles, and Olga Roller.
THEIR MUSICAL NUMBERS: 'I Can't Make My Feet Behave', 'Squab Farm', 'Bring On the Girls', 'Twit, Twit, Twit', and 'Quick Service'.

APPLE BLOSSOMS
Opened 7 October, 1919, at the Globe Theatre, Broadway: 256 performances

Produced by Charles Dillingham. Directed by Fred C. Latham. Music directed by William Daly. Book and lyrics by William LeBaron. Music by Fritz Kreisler and Victor Jacobi. Dance director: Edward Royce. Settings: Joseph Urban.

WITH John Charles Thomas, Wilda Bennett, Roy Atwell, Rena Parker, Percival Knight, Juanita Fletcher, Alan Fagan, Harrison Brockbank, and Florence Shirley.
THEIR MUSICAL NUMBERS: 'On the Banks of the Bronx' and 'A Girl, a Man, a Night, a Dance'.

THE LOVE LETTER
Opened 4 October, 1921, at the Globe Theatre, Broadway: 31 performances

Produced by Charles Dillingham. Directed by Edward Royce, who also directed the dance sequences. Music directed by William Daly. Book and lyrics by William LeBaron. Music by Victor Jacobi. Settings: Joseph Urban.

WITH John Charles Thomas, Carolyn Thomson, Alice Brady, Marjorie Gateson, Will West, Bessie Franklin, and Jane Carroll.
THEIR MUSICAL NUMBERS: 'I'll Say I Love You', 'Upside Down', and 'Dreaming'.

FOR GOODNESS SAKE

Opened 20 February, 1922, at the Lyric Theatre, Broadway: 103 performances

Produced by Alex A. Aarons. Directed by Priestley Morrison. Music directed by William Daly. Lyrics by Arthur Jackson. Music by William Daly and Paul Lannin. Book by Fred Jackson. Dance director: Allan K. Foster. Settings: P. Dodd Ackerman.

WITH John E. Hazzard, Marjorie Gateson, Charles Judels, Vinton Freedley, and Helen Ford.

THEIR MUSICAL NUMBERS: 'All to Myself', 'When You're in Rome', 'Oh Gee, Oh Gosh', 'French Pastry Walk', and 'The Whichness of the Whatness'.

THE BUNCH AND JUDY

Opened 28 November, 1922, at the Globe Theatre, Broadway: 65 performances

Produced by Charles Dillingham. Directed by Fred G. Latham. Music directed by Victor Baravalle. Lyrics by Anne Caldwell. Music by Jerome Kern. Book by Anne Caldwell and Hugh Ford. Settings: Gates and Morange.

WITH Johnny Dooley, Ray Dooley, Grace Hayes, Roberta Beatty, Philip Tonge, 6 Brown Brothers, Carl McBride, Augustus Minton, and Patricia Clark.

THEIR MUSICAL NUMBERS: 'Pale Venetian Moon', 'Peach Girl', 'Morning Glory', 'Every Day in Every Way', 'Times Square', and 'How Do You Do, Katinka?'.

Over the Top   *Inset:* The Passing Show of 1918

Funny Face

STOP FLIRTING
Opened 30 May, 1923, at the Shaftesbury Theatre, London: 418 performances

Produced by Alfred Butt. Directed by Felix Edwardes. Music directed by Jacques Heuvel. Dance director: Gus Sohlke. Settings: Phil Harker.

WITH Jack Melford, Mimi Crawford, Marjorie Gordon, Henry Kendall, and George de Warfaz.
THEIR MUSICAL NUMBERS: 'All to Myself', 'I'll Build a Stairway to Paradise', 'Oh Gee, Oh Gosh', 'It's Great to Be in Love', and 'The Whichness of the Whatness'.

LADY, BE GOOD!
Opened 1 December, 1924, at the Liberty Theatre, Broadway: 330 performances

Produced by Alex A. Aarons and Vinton Freedley. Directed by Felix Edwardes. Music directed by Paul Lannin. Lyrics by Ira Gershwin. Music by George Gershwin. Book by Guy Bolton and Fred Thompson. Settings: Norman Bel Geddes.

WITH Walter Catlett, Alan Edwards, Cliff Edwards, Gerald Oliver Smith, Kathlene Martin, Patricia Clark, and Phil Ohman and Vic Arden (duo-pianists).
THEIR MUSICAL NUMBERS: 'Hang on to Me', 'So Am I', 'Fascinating Rhythm', 'The Half of It, Dearie, Blues', 'Juanita', and 'Swiss Miss'.

LADY, BE GOOD!
Opened 14 April, 1926, at the Empire Theatre, London: 326 performances

Produced by Alfred Butt, with Alex A. Aarons and Vinton Freedley. Directed by Felix Edwardes. Music directed by Jacques Heuvel. Dance director: Max Scheck. Settings: Joseph and Phil Harker.

WITH William Kent, Buddy Lee, George Vollaire, Ewart Scott, Sylvia Leslie, Glori Beaumont, and Irene Russell.
THEIR MUSICAL NUMBERS: 'Hang on to Me', 'Fascinating Rhythm', 'So Am I', 'I'd Rather Charleston', 'The Half of It, Dearie, Blues', 'Juanita', and 'Swiss Miss'.

FUNNY FACE
Opened 22 November, 1927, at the Alvin Theatre, Broadway: 250 performances

Produced by Alex A. Aarons and Vinton Freedley. Directed by Edgar MacGregor. Music directed by Alfred Newman. Lyrics by Ira Gershwin. Music by George Gershwin. Book by Fred Thompson and Paul Gerald Smith. Dance director: Bobby Connolly. Settings: John Wenger.

WITH William Kent, Victor Moore, Allen Kearns, Betty Compton, Ritz Quartette, Gertrude McDonald, Dorothy Jordan, and Phil Ohman and Vic Arden (duo-pianists).
THEIR MUSICAL NUMBERS: 'Funny Face', 'High Hat', 'He Loves and She Loves', 'Let's Kiss and Make Up', ''S Wonderful', 'My One and Only', and 'The Babbitt and the Bromide'.

FUNNY FACE

Opened 8 November, 1928, at the Prince's Theatre, London: 263 performances

Produced by Alfred Butt and Lee Ephraim with Alex A. Aarons and Vinton Freedley. Directed by Felix Edwardes. Music directed by Julian Jones. Dance director: Bobby Connolly. Settings: Joseph and Phil Harker.

WITH Leslie Henson, Bernard Clifton, Rita Page, Sydney Howard, Eilen Hatton, and Jacques Frey and Mario Braggiotti (duo-pianists).
THEIR MUSICAL NUMBERS: 'Funny Face', 'High Hat', ''S Wonderful', 'Let's Kiss and Make Up', 'Imagination', 'My One and Only', and 'The Babbitt and the Bromide'.

SMILES

Opened 18 November, 1930, at the Ziegfeld Theatre, Broadway: 63 performances

Produced by Florenz Ziegfeld. Directed by William Anthony McGuire. Music directed by Frank Tours. Lyrics by Clifford Grey, Harold Adamson, and Ring Lardner. Music by Vincent Youmans. Book by William Anthony McGuire. Dance director: Ned Wayburn. Settings: Joseph Urban.

WITH Marilyn Miller, Tom Howard, Eddie Foy Jr, Paul Gregory, Larry Adler, Claire Dodd, Georgia Caine, Edward Raquello, Kathryn Hereford, Adrian Rosley, Aber Twins, Bob Hope, and Virginia Bruce.
THEIR MUSICAL NUMBERS: 'Say, Young Man of Manhattan', 'Hotcha Ma Chotch', 'Be Good to Me', 'Anyway, We Had Fun', 'If I Were You, Love', and 'I'm Glad I Waited'.

THE BAND WAGON

Opened 3 June, 1931, at the New Amsterdam Theatre, Broadway: 260 performances

Produced by Max Gordon, Directed by Hassard Short. Music directed by Al Goodman. Lyrics by Howard Dietz. Music by Arthur Schwartz. Sketches by George S. Kaufman and Howard Dietz. Dance director: Albertina Rasch. Settings: Albert Johnston.

WITH Frank Morgan, Helen Broderick, Tilly Losch, Philip Loeb, John Barker, Roberta Robinson, Francis Pierlot, Jay Wilson, and Peter Chambers.
THEIR MUSICAL NUMBERS: 'Sweet Music', 'Hoops', 'New Sun in the Sky', 'Miserable with You', 'I Love Louisa', 'The Beggar Waltz', and 'White Heat'.

GAY DIVORCE

Opened 29 November, 1932, at the Ethel Barrymore Theatre, Broadway: 248 performances

Produced by Dwight Deere Wiman and Tom Weatherly. Directed by Howard Lindsay. Music directed by Gene Salzer. Lyrics and music by Cole Porter. Book by Dwight Taylor. Dance directors: Carl Randall and Barbara Newberry. Settings: Jo Mielziner.

WITH Claire Luce, Luella Gear, G. P. Huntley Jr, Betty Starbuck, Erik Rhodes, Eric Blore, and Roland Bottomley.
HIS MUSICAL NUMBERS: 'After You, Who?' 'Night and Day', 'I've Got You on My Mind', and 'You're in Love'.

GAY DIVORCE

Opened 2 November, 1933, at the Palace Theatre, London: 108 performances

Produced by Lee Ephraim. Directed by Felix Edwardes. Music directed by Percival Mackey. Dance directors: Carl Randall and Barbara Newberry. Settings: Joseph and Phil Harker.

WITH Claire Luce, Olive Blakeney, Claud Allister, Eric Blore, Joan Gardner, Erik Rhodes, and Fred Hearne.
HIS MUSICAL NUMBERS: 'After You, Who?', 'Night and Day', 'I've Got You on My Mind', and 'You're in Love'.

FILMOGRAPHY

DANCING LADY
Metro–Goldwyn–Mayer 1933

Produced by David O. Selznick. Directed by Robert Z. Leonard. Music directed by Louis Silvers. Screenplay by Allen Rivkin and P. J. Wolfson from the novel by James Warner Bellah. Lyrics by Harold Adamson, Dorothy Fields, Lorenz Hart, and Arthur Freed. Music by Burton Lane, Jimmy McHugh, Richard Rodgers, and Nacio Herb Brown. Dance directors: Sammy Lee and Eddie Prinz. Art director: Merrill Pye. Running time: 90 minutes.

WITH Joan Crawford, Clark Gable, and Franchot Tone. Also features Nelson Eddy and Robert Benchley.
ASTAIRE plays himself in an archetypal backstage plot with Crawford as a chorus girl who becomes a star and Gable as her producer.
HIS MUSICAL NUMBERS: 'Heigh-Ho, the Gang's All Here' (Adamson–Lane) song with chorus and Crawford; dance with Crawford. 'Let's Go Bavarian' (Adamson–Lane) song with chorus and Crawford.

FLYING DOWN TO RIO
RKO Radio Pictures 1933

Produced by Louis Brock. Directed by Thornton Freeland. Music directed by Max Steiner. Screenplay by Cyril Hume, H. W. Hanemann, and Erwin Gelsey from the play by Anne Caldwell, based on a story by Louis Brock. Lyrics by Edward Eliscu and Gus Kahn. Music by Vincent Youmans. Dance director: Dave Gould. Assistant: Hermes Pan. Art directors: Van Nest Polglase and Carroll Clark. Running time 89 minutes.

WITH Dolores Del Rio, Gene Raymond, Raul Roulien, and Ginger Rogers. Also features Eric Blore.
ASTAIRE, as dancer, and Rogers, band vocalist, help bandleader-aviator Raymond win Del Rio's love by staging an exciting aerial opening for her father's new hotel.
HIS MUSICAL NUMBERS: 'The Carioca' dance with Rogers, supported by Brazilians and The Turunas; song by Etta Moten and two unbilled singers. 'Orchids in the Moonlight' dance with Del Rio; song by Roulien. 'Flying Down to Rio' song; dance by aerial chorus.

Dancing Lady

Flying Down To Rio

THE GAY DIVORCEE
GB: THE GAY DIVORCE
RKO Radio Pictures 1934

Produced by Pandro S. Berman. Directed by Mark Sandrich. Music directed by Max Steiner. Screenplay by George Marion Jr, Dorothy Yost, and Edward Kaufman from the stage musical, *Gay Divorce*, by Dwight Taylor. Lyrics by Cole Porter, Herb Magidson, and Mack Gordon. Music by Cole Porter, Con Conrad, and Harry Revel. Dance director: Dave Gould. Art directors: Van Nest Polglase and Carroll Clark. Running time: 107 minutes.

WITH Ginger Rogers, Alice Brady, Edward Everett Horton, Erik Rhodes, and Eric Blore. Also features Betty Grable in a minor role. ASTAIRE plays a dancer whom Rogers mistakes for the professional co-respondent with whom she plans to establish grounds for her divorce.
HIS MUSICAL NUMBERS: 'Don't Let It Bother You' (Gordon–Revel) dance; song by French chorus. 'A Needle in a Haystack' (Magidson–Conrad) song and dance. 'Night and Day' (Porter) song; dance with Rogers. 'The Continental' (Magidson–Conrad) dance with Rogers, and chorus; song by Rogers, Rhodes, and Lillian Miles.

ROBERTA
RKO Radio Pictures 1935

Produced by Pandro S. Berman. Directed by William A. Seiter. Music directed by Max Steiner. Screenplay by Jane Murfin, Sam Mintz, Glenn Tryon, and Allan Scott from the stage musical, *Roberta*, by Otto Harbach, adapted from the novel, *Gowns by Roberta*, by Alice Duer Miller. Lyrics by Otto Harbach, Dorothy Fields, Ballard Macdonald, Bernard Dougall and Oscar Hammerstein II. Music by Jerome Kern and James F. Hanley. Dance director: Hermes Pan. Art directors: Van Nest Polglase and Carroll Clark. Running time: 105 minutes.

WITH Irene Dunne, Ginger Rogers, Randolph Scott, and Helen Westley.
ASTAIRE and nightclub singer Rogers help Scott make a big success with the Paris fashion house he inherits from his aunt.
HIS MUSICAL NUMBERS: 'Let's Begin' (Harbach–Kern) song with Candy Candido; dance with Candido and Gene Sheldon. 'I'll Be Hard to Handle' (Dougall–Kern) dance with Rogers; song by Rogers. 'I Won't Dance' (Fields–Kern) song with Rogers; piano playing and dance. 'Smoke Gets in Your Eyes' (Harbach–Kern) dance reprise with Rogers; song by Dunne. 'Don't Ask Me Not to Sing'; song with models. 'Lovely to Look At' (Fields–Kern) song reprise and dance with Rogers; song by Dunne and male chorus.

TOP HAT
RKO Radio Pictures 1935

Produced by Pandro S. Berman. Directed by Mark Sandrich. Music directed by Max Steiner. Screenplay by Dwight Taylor and Allan Scott from the play, *The Girl Who Dared*, by Alexander Farago and Aladar Laszlo. Lyrics and music by Irving Berlin. Dance director: Hermes Pan. Art director: Van Nest Polglase. Running time: 101 minutes.

WITH Ginger Rogers, Edward Everett Horton, Helen Broderick, Erik Rhodes, and Eric Blore. ASTAIRE plays an American dancer who falls for Rogers and follows her to Venice, ultimately rescuing her from a rebound marriage she enters believing him to be her best friend's husband.
HIS MUSICAL NUMBERS: 'No Strings' song and dance. 'Isn't This a Lovely Day?' song; dance with Rogers. 'Top Hat, White Tie and Tails' song; dance, with male chorus. 'Cheek to Cheek' song; dance with Rogers. 'The Piccolino' dance with Rogers, and chorus; song by Rogers.

The Gay Divorcee

Top Hat

Follow the Fleet

FOLLOW THE FLEET
RKO Radio Pictures 1936

Produced by Pandro S. Berman. Directed by
Mark Sandrich. Music directed by Max Steiner.
Screenplay by Dwight Taylor and Allan Scott
from the play, *Shore Leave*, by Hubert Osborne.
Lyrics and music by Irving Berlin. Dance director:
Hermes Pan. Art director: Van Nest Polglase.
Running time: 110 minutes.

WITH Ginger Rogers, Randolph Scott, and Harriet
Hilliard. Also features Lucille Ball and Betty
Grable in minor roles.
ASTAIRE as dancer turned sailor raises the money to
salvage a ship by putting on a show with Rogers,
his one-time partner.
HIS MUSICAL NUMBERS: 'We Saw the Sea' song
with sailors. 'Let Yourself Go' dance with Rogers,
Dorothy Fleisman and Bob Cromer, and others,
reprised by Rogers; song by Rogers with Grable,
Joy Hodges, and Jennie Gray. 'I'd Rather Lead a
Band' song; dance with sailors. 'I'm Putting All
My Eggs in One Basket' song and dance with
Rogers; piano playing. 'Let's Face the Music and
Dance' song; dance with Rogers.

SWING TIME
RKO Radio Pictures 1936

Produced by Pandro S. Berman. Directed by
George Stevens. Music directed by Nathaniel
Shilkret. Screenplay by Howard Lindsay and
Allan Scott from the story, *Portrait of John Garnett*,
by Erwin Gelsey. Lyrics by Dorothy Fields. Music
by Jerome Kern. Dance director: Hermes Pan. Art
director: Van Nest Polglase. Running time: 103
minutes.

WITH Ginger Rogers, Victor Moore, Helen
Broderick, Eric Blore, Betty Furness, and Georges
Metaxa.
ASTAIRE is a dancer-gambler in New York to make
his fortune who falls for dancing-instructor Rogers
and abandons his plans to marry the girl back home.

HIS MUSICAL NUMBERS: 'It's Not in the Cards'
dance with troupe. 'Pick Yourself Up' song with
Rogers; dance with Rogers, Moore, and
Broderick. 'The Way You Look Tonight' song.
'Waltz in Swing Time' dance with Rogers. 'A
Fine Romance' song with Rogers. 'Bojangles of
Harlem' dance with chorus; song by chorus.
'Never Gonna Dance' song; dance with Rogers.

SHALL WE DANCE
RKO Radio Pictures 1937

Produced by Pandro S. Berman. Directed by
Mark Sandrich. Music directed by Nathaniel
Shilkret. Screenplay by Allan Scott and Ernest
Pagano from the story, *Watch Your Step*, by Lee
Loeb and Harold Buchman. Lyrics by Ira
Gershwin. Music by George Gershwin. Dance
directors: Hermes Pan and Harry Losee. Art
director: Van Nest Polglase. Running time: 116
minutes.

WITH Ginger Rogers, Edward Everett Horton,
Eric Blore, and Harriet Hoctor.
ASTAIRE is a ballet dancer who falls for musical-
comedy star Rogers. Rumours that they are
husband and wife force them into marriage.
HIS MUSICAL NUMBERS: 'Beginner's Luck' dance.
'Slap that Bass' song with unbilled singer; dance.
'They All Laughed' dance with Rogers; song by
Rogers. 'Let's Call the Whole Thing Off' song and
dance with Rogers. 'They Can't Take That Away
from Me' song; dance reprise with Hoctor. 'Shall
We Dance' song; dance with Rogers, and chorus.

Shall We Dance

Swing Time

A DAMSEL IN DISTRESS
RKO Radio Pictures 1937

Produced by Pandro S. Berman. Directed by George Stevens. Music directed by Victor Baravalle. Screenplay by P. G. Wodehouse, Ernest Pagano, and S. K. Lauren from the novel by P. G. Wodehouse, and the play by Wodehouse and Ian Hay. Lyrics by Ira Gershwin. Music by George Gershwin. Dance director: Hermes Pan. Art director: Van Nest Polglase. Running time: 100 minutes.

WITH George Burns, Gracie Allen, Joan Fontaine, Reginald Gardiner, and Constance Collier.
ASTAIRE loves Fontaine, a rich English lady with a castle and a sinister butler. Burns and Allen 'help' him rescue her.
HIS MUSICAL NUMBERS: 'I Can't Be Bothered Now' song and dance. 'The Jolly Tar and the Milkmaid' song with madrigal singers. 'Put Me to the Test' dance with Burns and Allen. 'Stiff Upper Lip' dance with Burns and Allen, and fairgoers; song by Allen. 'Things Are Looking Up' song; stroll with Fontaine. 'A Foggy Day' song. 'Nice Work If You Can Get It' song with Betty Duggan, Mary Dean, Pearl Amatore; drum solo and dance reprise.

A Damsel in Distress

CAREFREE
RKO Radio Pictures 1938

Produced by Pandro S. Berman. Directed by Mark Sandrich. Music directed by Victor Baravalle. Screenplay by Ernest Pagano and Allan Scott from a story by Marian Ainslee and Guy Endore. Lyrics and music by Irving Berlin. Dance director: Hermes Pan. Art director: Van Nest Polglase. Running time: 83 minutes.

WITH Ginger Rogers and Ralph Bellamy.
ASTAIRE is a psychiatrist determined to persuade radio singer Rogers that she loves him, not the man she's engaged to.
HIS MUSICAL NUMBERS: 'Since They Turned Loch Lomond into Swing' harmonica playing, golf-club wielding, and dance. 'I Used to be Colour Blind' song; dance with Rogers. 'The Yam' dance with Rogers; song by Rogers. 'Change Partners' song; dance with Rogers.

THE STORY OF VERNON AND IRENE CASTLE
RKO Radio Pictures 1939

Produced by George Haight. Directed by H. C. Potter. Music directed by Victor Baravalle. Screenplay by Richard Sherman, Oscar Hammerstein II, and Dorothy Yost from the book, *My Husband*, by Irene Castle. Dance director: Hermes Pan. Art director: Van Nest Polglase. Running time: 90 minutes.

WITH Ginger Rogers, Edna May Oliver, Walter Brennan, and Lew Fields. Also features Marge Champion in a minor role.
ASTAIRE plays Vernon Castle, top ballroom dancer until his death in a wartime aircrash. Rogers is his partner, Irene.
HIS MUSICAL NUMBERS: 'By the Light of the Silvery Moon' (Madden–Edwards) dance. 'Only When You're in My Arms (Conrad, Kalmar, Ruby) song. 'Waiting for the Robert E. Lee' (Gilbert–Muir) dance with Rogers. 'Too Much Mustard' (Macklin) dance with Rogers. 'Rose Room' (Williams–Hickman) dance with Rogers. 'Très Jolie' (Waldteufel) dance with Rogers. 'When They Were Dancing Around' (McCarthy–Monaco) dance with Rogers. 'Little Brown Jug' (Winner) dance with Rogers. 'Dengozo' (Nazareth) dance with Rogers. Medley including 'You're Here and I'm Here' (Smith–Kern), 'Chicago' (Fisher), 'Hello, Frisco, Hello' (Buck–Hirsch), 'Way Down Yonder in New Orleans' (Creamer–Layton), and 'Take Me Back to New York Town' (Sterling-Von Tilzer) dance with Rogers. 'Hello, Hello, Who's Your Lady Friend?' (David–Lee) song; dance, with soldiers. Medley including 'Destiny Waltz' (Baynes), 'Night of Gladness' (Ancliffe), and 'Missouri Waltz' (Royce–Logan) dance with Rogers.

The Story of Vernon and Irene Castle

Carefree

BROADWAY MELODY OF 1940
Metro–Goldwyn–Mayer 1940

Produced by Jack Cummings. Directed by Norman Taurog. Music directed by Alfred Newman. Screenplay by Leon Gordon and George Oppenheimer from the story by Jack MacGowan and Dore Schary. Lyrics and music by Cole Porter. Dance director: Bobby Connolly. Art director: Cedric Gibbons. Running time: 102 minutes.

WITH Eleanor Powell, George Murphy, Frank Morgan, and Ian Hunter.
ASTAIRE plays half a down-at-heel dancing team. In a confusion over names, his partner, Murphy, is mistakenly chosen to dance in a Broadway show opposite Powell.
HIS MUSICAL NUMBER: 'Please Don't Monkey with Broadway' song and dance with Murphy. 'I've Got My Eyes on You' song, dance, and piano playing. 'Jukebox Dance' dance with Powell. 'I Concentrate on You' dance with Powell; song by Douglas McPhail. 'Begin the Beguine' dance with Powell, and chorus; unbilled singers.

Broadway Melody of 1940

You'll Never Get Rich

SECOND CHORUS
Paramount 1940

Produced by Boris Morros. Directed by H. C. Potter. Music directed by Ed Paul. Screenplay by Elaine Ryan and Ian McClellan Hunter from the story by Fred Cavett. Lyrics by Johnny Mercer, Will Harris, and E. Y. Harbourg. Music by Artie Shaw, Bernard Hanighen, Hal Borne, Victor Young, and Johnny Green. Dance director: Hermes Pan. Art director: Boris Leven. Running time: 84 minutes.

WITH Paulette Goddard, Artie Shaw, Burgess Meredith (trumpet playing by Billy Butterfield), and Charles Butterworth. Astaire's trumpet playing by Bobby Hackett.
ASTAIRE is a jazz trumpeter competing with Meredith for a job with Artie Shaw and Goddard's love.
HIS MUSICAL NUMBERS: 'I Ain't Hep to That Step but I'll Dig It' (Mercer–Borne) song; dance with Goddard. 'Love of My Life' (Mercer–Shaw) song with Shaw Orchestra. 'Poor Mr Chisholm' (Mercer–Hanighen) song; dance reprise, with Shaw Orchestra

YOU'LL NEVER GET RICH
Columbia 1941

Produced by Samuel Bischoff. Directed by Sidney Lanfield. Music directed by Morris Stoloff. Screenplay by Michael Fessier and Ernest Pagano. Lyrics and music by Cole Porter. Dance director: Robert Alton. Art director: Lionel Banks. Running time: 88 minutes.

WITH Rita Hayworth and Robert Benchley.
ASTAIRE is a dance director turned soldier in World War II who romances chorus-girl Hayworth.
HIS MUSICAL NUMBERS: 'The Boogie Barcarolle' dance with Hayworth, and chorus. 'Shootin' the Works for Uncle Sam' song and dance, with chorus. 'Since I Kissed My Baby Goodbye' dance; song by Delta Rhythm Boys. 'A-stairable Rag' dance, with jazz group. 'So Near and Yet So Far' song; dance with Hayworth. 'Wedding Cake Walk' dance with Hayworth, and chorus; song by Martha Tilton.

Second Chorus

HOLIDAY INN
Paramount 1942

Produced and directed by Mark Sandrich. Music directed by Robert Emmett Dolan. Screenplay by Claude Binyon and Elmer Rice from an idea by Irving Berlin. Lyrics and music by Irving Berlin. Dance director: Danny Dare. Art directors: Hans Dreier and Roland Anderson. Running time: 100 minutes.

WITH Bing Crosby, Marjorie Reynolds (sung by Martha Mears), and Virginia Dale.
ASTAIRE is a dancer in this story of professional and romantic regroupings played out at Crosby's holidays-only nightclub.
HIS MUSICAL NUMBERS: 'I'll Capture Your Heart Singing' song with Crosby and Dale. 'You're Easy to Dance With' song, with chorus; dance with Dale; dance reprise with Reynolds. 'Be Careful, It's My Heart' dance with Reynolds; song by Crosby. 'I Can't Tell a Lie' song; dance with Reynolds, with Bob Cats. 'Let's Say It with Firecrackers' dance; song by chorus.

YOU WERE NEVER LOVELIER
Columbia Pictures 1942

Produced by Louis F. Edelman. Directed by William A. Seiter. Music directed by Leigh Harline. Screenplay by Michael Fessier, Ernest Pagano, and Delmar Daves from a story by Carlos Oliveri and Sixto Pondal Rios. Lyrics by Johnny Mercer. Music by Jerome Kern. Dance director: Val Raset. Art director: Lionel Banks. Running time: 98 minutes.

WITH Rita Hayworth (sung by Nan Wynn), Adolphe Menjou, and Xavier Cugat.
ASTAIRE is a dancer-gambler who wins the hand of Buenos Aires hotelier's daughter, Hayworth.
HIS MUSICAL NUMBERS: 'Dearly Beloved' song, with Cugat Orchestra, reprised by Hayworth; dance by Hayworth. 'Audition Dance' dance, with Cugat Orchestra. 'I'm Old Fashioned' dance with Hayworth; song by Hayworth. 'Shorty George' song, with Cugat Orchestra; dance with Hayworth. 'You Were Never Lovelier' song; dance with Hayworth.

THE SKY'S THE LIMIT
RKO Radio Pictures 1943

Produced by David Hempstead. Directed by Edward H. Griffith. Music directed by Leigh Harline. Screenplay by Frank Fenton and Lynn Root. Lyrics by Johnny Mercer. Music by Harold Arlen. Dance director: Fred Astaire. Art directors: Albert S. D'Agostino and Carroll Clark. Running time: 89 minutes.

WITH Joan Leslie (sung by Sally Sweetland), Robert Benchley, Robert Ryan, and Eric Blore.
ASTAIRE plays a member of the elite Flying Tigers Airforce Corp who skips the hero's tour arranged for him and meets singer Leslie in a serviceman's canteen.
HIS MUSICAL NUMBERS: 'My Shining Hour' song reprise, song by Leslie, with Slack Orchestra; dance reprise with Leslie. 'A Lot in Common with You' song and dance with Leslie. 'One For My Baby' song and dance.

You Were Never Lovelier

Holiday Inn

The Sky's the Limit

YOLANDA AND THE THIEF

Metro–Goldwyn–Mayer 1945
Technicolor

Produced by Arthur Freed. Directed by Vincente Minnelli. Music directed by Lennie Hayton. Screenplay by Irving Brecher from the story by Jacques Thery and Ludwig Bemelmans. Lyrics by Arthur Freed. Music by Harry Warren. Dance director: Eugene Loring. Art directors: Cedric Gibbons and Jack Martin Smith. Running time: 108 minutes.

WITH Lucille Bremer (sung by Trudy Erwin) and Frank Morgan.
ASTAIRE plays a conman, who with friend Morgan tries to persuade a South American heiress that he is her guardian angel.
HIS MUSICAL NUMBERS: 'Dream Ballet' dance with Bremer and chorus; song by Bremer, with chorus. 'Yolanda' song; dance. 'Coffee Time' dance with Bremer; song by chorus.

Yolanda and the Thief

ZIEGFELD FOLLIES

Metro–Goldwyn–Mayer 1946
Technicolor

Produced by Arthur Freed. Directed by Vincente Minnelli. Music directed by Lennie Hayton. Dance director: Robert Alton. Art directors: Cedric Gibbons, Merrill Pye, and Jack Martin Smith. Running time: 110 minutes.

WITH Lucille Ball, Lucille Bremer, Fanny Brice, Judy Garland, Kathryn Grayson, Lena Horne, Gene Kelly, James Melton, Victor Moore, Red Skelton, Esther Williams, William Powell, Edward Arnold, Marion Bell, Bunin's Puppets, Cyd Charisse, Hume Cronyn, William Frawley, Robert Lewis, Virginia O'Brien, Keenan Wynn, Grady Sutton, Rex Evans, Charles Coleman, Joseph Crehan, Harry Hayden, Eddie Dunn, William B. Davidson, Gary Owen, Harrier Lee, and Rod Alexander.
ASTAIRE introduces this tribute to Florenz Ziegfeld.
HIS MUSICAL NUMBERS: 'Here's to the Girls' (Freed–Edens) song, with chorus; whip-cracking by Ball, dance by Charisse, with chorus. 'This Heart of Mine' (Freed–Warren) song, with chorus; dance with Bremer. 'Limehouse Blues' (Furber–Braham) dance with Bremer; song by Lee. 'The Babbitt and the Bromide' (I. Gershwin–G. Gershwin) song and dance with Kelly.

BLUE SKIES

Paramount 1946
Technicolor

Produced by Sol C. Siegel. Directed by Stuart Heisler. Music directed by Robert Emmett Dolan. Screenplay by Arthur Sheekman and Allan Scott. Lyrics and music by Irving Berlin. Dance director: Hermes Pan. Art directors: Hans Dreier and Hal Pereira. Running time: 104 minutes.

WITH Bing Crosby, Joan Caulfield, Billy De Wolfe, and Olga San Juan.
ASTAIRE loves Caulfield who instead marries Crosby. The marriage fails and Caulfield returns to Astaire, but is finally re-united with Crosby.
HIS MUSICAL NUMBERS: 'A Pretty Girl is Like a Melody' dance; song by chorus. 'Putting on the Ritz' song and dance. 'A Couple of Song and Dance Men' song and dance with Crosby. 'Heat Wave' dance with San Juan and chorus; song by San Juan and chorus.

Ziegfeld Follies

EASTER PARADE
Metro–Goldwyn–Mayer 1948
Technicolor

Produced by Arthur Freed. Directed by Charles
Walters. Music directed by Johnny Green.
Screenplay by Sidney Sheldon, Frances Goodrich,
and Albert Hackett. Lyrics and music by Irving
Berlin. Dance director: Robert Alton. Art
directors: Cedric Gibbons and Jack Martin Smith.
Running time: 103 minutes.

WITH Judy Garland, Peter Lawford, Ann Miller.
ASTAIRE plays a tap dancer who, after his partner
deserts him, transforms Garland from unsuccessful
chorus-girl to star and then falls in love with her.
HIS MUSICAL NUMBERS: 'Happy Easter' song with
chorus. 'Drum Crazy' song and dance. 'It Only
Happens When I Dance With You' song; reprise
by Garland; dance with Miller. 'Beautiful Faces
Need Beautiful Clothes' dance with Garland. 'I
Love a Piano' dance with Garland; song by
Garland. 'Snooky Ookums' song with Garland.
'Ragtime Violin' song; dance with Garland.
'When the Midnight Choo-Choo Leaves for
Alabam'' song and dance with Garland. 'Steppin'
Out with My Baby' song with chorus; dance with
Pat Jackson. 'A Couple of Swells' song and dance
with Garland. 'Easter Parade' song with Garland
and chorus.

The Barkleys of Broadway

Easter Parade

THE BARKLEYS OF BROADWAY
Metro–Goldwyn–Mayer 1949
Technicolor

Produced by Arthur Freed. Directed by Charles
Walters. Music directed by Lennie Hayton.
Screenplay by Betty Comden and Adolph Green.
Lyrics by Ira Gershwin and Arthur Freed. Music
by Harry Warren. Dance directors: Robert Alton
and Hermes Pan. Art directors: Cedric Gibbons
and Edward Carfagno. Running time: 109 minutes.

WITH Ginger Rogers and Oscar Levant.
ASTAIRE and Rogers play a successful married
double act who fight when Rogers wants to leave
musicals for drama.
HIS MUSICAL NUMBERS: 'Swing Trot' dance with
Rogers. 'You'd Be Hard to Replace' song.
'Bouncin' the Blues' dance with Rogers. 'My One
and Only Highland Fling' song and dance with
Rogers. 'A Weekend in the Country' song with
Rogers and Levant. 'Shoes with Wings On' song
and dance. 'They Can't Take That Away from
Me' (G. Gershwin–I. Gershwin) song; dance with
Rogers. 'Manhattan Downbeat' song with chorus;
dance with Rogers and chorus.

LET'S DANCE
Paramount 1950
Technicolor

Produced by Robert Fellows. Directed by
Norman Z. McLeod. Music directed by Robert
Emmett Dolan. Screenplay by Allan Scott and
Dane Lussier from the story, *Little Boy Blue*, by
Maurice Zolotow. Lyrics and music by Frank
Loesser. Dance director: Hermes Pan. Art
directors: Hans Dreier and Roland Anderson.
Running time: 111 minutes.

WITH Betty Hutton, Roland Young, Ruth
Warwick, and Lucile Watson.
ASTAIRE helps former partner Hutton in her battle
to keep her son from being taken away by her
mother-in-law.
HIS MUSICAL NUMBERS: 'Can't Stop Talking' song
with Hutton. 'Piano Dance' dance. 'Jack and the
Beanstalk' song. 'Oh, Them Dudes' song and
dance with Hutton. 'Why Fight the Feeling' dance
with Hutton; song by Hutton. 'The Hyacinth'
dance with Watson. 'Tunnel of Love' song and
dance with Hutton.

Let's Dance

163

THREE LITTLE WORDS
Metro–Goldwyn–Mayer 1950
Technicolor

Produced by Jack Cummings. Directed by Richard Thorpe. Music directed by André Previn. Screenplay by George Wells. Lyrics by Bert Kalmar, Edgar Leslie, and Arthur Freed. Music by Harry Ruby, Herman Ruby, Ted Snyder, Harry Puck, Herbert Stothart, and Nacio Herb Brown. Dance director: Hermes Pan. Art directors: Cedric Gibbons and Urie McCleary. Running time: 103 minutes.

WITH Red Skelton, Vera-Ellen, Arlene Dahl, and Keenan Wynn. Also features Debbie Reynolds. ASTAIRE and Skelton in a biopic of the songwriters Bert Kalmar and Harry Ruby.
HIS MUSICAL NUMBERS: 'Where Did You Get That Girl?' song with Anita Ellis (for Ellen); dance with Ellen. 'Mr and Mrs Hoofer at Home' dance with Ellen. 'My Sunny Tennessee' song with Skelton. 'So-Long-Oo-Long' song with Skelton. 'Nevertheless' song with Ellis (for Ellen); dance with Ellen. 'I Wanna Be Loved by You' song with Helen Kane (for Reynolds). 'Thinking of You' dance; song by Ellis (for Ellen); reprise by Dahl. 'Hooray for Captain Spaulding' song with Skelton. 'Three Little Words' song; reprise by Phil Regan.

ROYAL WEDDING
GB: WEDDING BELLS
Metro–Goldwyn–Meyer 1951
Technicolor

Produced by Arthur Freed. Directed by Stanley Donen. Music directed by Johnny Green. Screenplay by Alan Jay Lerner. Lyrics by Alan Jay Lerner. Music by Burton Lane. Dance director: Nick Castle. Art directors: Cedric Gibbons and Jack Martin Smith. Running time: 93 minutes.

WITH Jane Powell, Peter Lawford, Sarah Churchill, and Kennan Wynn.
ASTAIRE and Powell, his sister, are an American dance couple who both visit London, fall in love and marry on the same day as Princess Elizabeth and Philip Mountbatten.
HIS MUSICAL NUMBERS: 'Ev'ry Night at Seven' song; dance with Powell and chorus. 'Sunday Jumps' dance. 'Open Your Eyes' dance with Powell; song by Powell. 'How Could You Believe Me When I Said I Love You When You Know I've Been a Liar All My Life?' song and dance with Powell. 'You're All the World to Me' song and dance. 'I Left My Hat in Haiti' song with chorus; dance with Powell and chorus.

THE BELLE OF NEW YORK
Metro–Goldwyn–Mayer 1952
Technicolor

Produced by Arthur Freed. Directed by Charles Walters. Music directed by Adolph Deutsch. Screenplay by Robert O'Brien, Irving Elinson, and Chester Erskine from a stage musical by Hugh Morton (C. M. S. McLennan) and Gustave Kerker. Lyrics by Johnny Mercer. Music by Harry Warren. Dance director: Robert Alton. Art directors: Cedric Gibbons and Jack Martin Smith. Running time: 82 minutes.

WITH Vera-Ellen (sung by Anita Ellis), Marjorie Main, Keenan Wynn, and Alice Pearce.
ASTAIRE is a rake who falls for a prim salvationist in the early 1900s.
HIS MUSICAL NUMBERS: 'When I'm Out with the Belle of New York' dance with Ellen; song by chorus. 'Bachelor Dinner Song' song and dance. 'Seeing's Believing' song and dance. 'Baby Doll' song; dance with Ellen. 'Oops' song; dance with Ellen. 'A Bride's Wedding Day Song' song by Ellen (sung by Ellis); dance with Ellen and chorus. 'I Wanna Be a Dancin' Man' song and dance.

Royal Wedding

The Belle of New York

Three Little Words

THE BAND WAGON
Metro–Goldwyn–Mayer 1953
Technicolor

Produced by Arthur Freed. Directed by Vincente Minnelli. Music directed by Adolph Deutsch. Screenplay by Betty Comden and Adolph Green. Lyrics by Howard Dietz. Music by Arthur Schwartz. Dance director: Michael Kidd. Art directors: Cedric Gibbons and Preston Ames. Running time: 111 minutes.

WITH Cyd Charisse, Oscar Levant, Nanette Fabray, and Jack Buchanan.
ASTAIRE plays an ageing dancer making a comeback with Charisse, a young ballet dancer, as his partner in a new Broadway musical. The show looks a certain flop, but is rescued at the last minute by the efforts of the cast.
HIS MUSICAL NUMBERS: 'By Myself' song. 'A Shine on Your Shoes' song; dance with LeRoy Daniels. 'That's Entertainment' song with Buchanan, Fabray and Levant; reprise by Charisse (sung by India Adams). 'Dancing in the Dark' dance with Charisse. 'You and the Night and the Music' dance with Charisse; song by chorus. 'I Love Louisa' song with Levant, Fabray and chorus. 'I Guess I'll Have to Change My Plan' song and dance with Buchanan. 'Triplets' song with Fabray and Buchanan. 'The Girl Hunt Ballet' (narration written by Alan Jay Lerner) spoken; dance with Charisse.

DADDY LONG LEGS
Twentieth Century–Fox 1955
Deluxe

Produced by Samuel G. Engel. Directed by Jean Negulesco. Music directed by Alfred Newman. Screenplay by Phoebe and Harry Ephron from a novel and play by Jean Webster. Lyrics and music by Johnny Mercer. Dance directors: David Robel and Roland Petit. Art directors: Lyle Wheeler and John DeCuir. Running time: 126 minutes.

WITH Leslie Caron, Terry Moore, Thelma Ritter, and Fred Clark.
ASTAIRE is the secret benefactor of orphan Caron who falls in love with him.

The Band Wagon

Daddy Long Legs

Funny Face

HIS MUSICAL NUMBERS: 'History of the Beat' song and dance. 'Daydream Sequence' dance with Caron and chorus. 'Dream' dance with Caron; song by chorus. 'Sluefoot' dance with Caron and chorus; song by chorus. 'Something's Gotta Give' song; dance with Caron. 'Dancing Through Life Ballet' dance with Caron and chorus.

FUNNY FACE
Paramount 1957
Technicolor

Produced by Roger Edens. Directed by Stanley Donen. Music directed by Adolph Deutsch. Screenplay by Leonard Gershe. Lyrics by Ira Gershwin and Leonard Gershe. Music by George Gershwin and Roger Edens. Dance director: Eugene Loring. Art directors: Hal Pereira and George W. Davis. Running time: 103 minutes.

WITH Audrey Hepburn, Kay Thomson, and Michel Auclair
ASTAIRE is a fashion photographer who transforms dowdy Hepburn into a top model. On assignment in Paris, the two fall in love.
HIS MUSICAL NUMBERS: 'Funny Face' song; dance with Hepburn. 'Bonjour Paris!' song with Thompson, Hepburn, and chorus. 'Let's Kiss and Make Up' song and dance. 'He Loves and She Loves' song; dance with Hepburn. 'Clap Yo' Hands' song with Thompson. ''S Wonderful' song and dance with Hepburn.

SILK STOCKINGS
Metro–Goldwyn–Mayer 1957
Metrocolor

Produced by Arthur Freed. Directed by Rouben Mamoulian. Music directed by André Previn. Screenplay by Leonard Gershe and Leonard Spigelgass, based on the story, *Ninotchka*, by Melchior Lengyal. Lyrics and music by Cole Porter. Dance directors: Hermes Pan and Eugene Loring. Art directors: William A. Horning and Randall Duell. Running time: 117 minutes.

WITH Cyd Charisse, Janis Paige, Peter Lorre, Jules Munshin, George Tobias, and Joseph Buloff.
ASTAIRE as an American businessman who visits Paris and falls in love with Charisse, a beautiful but severe Russian, whom he transforms.

HIS MUSICAL NUMBERS: 'Too Bad' song with Lorre, Munshin, Buloff, Betty Uitti, Barrie Chase, and Tybee Afra. 'Paris Loves Lovers' song with Carol Richards (for Charisse). 'Stereophonic Sound' song and dance with Paige. 'All of You' song; dance with Charisse. 'Fated to be Mated' song; dance with Charisse. 'The Ritz Roll and Rock' song; dance with chorus.

ON THE BEACH
United Artists 1959

Produced and directed by Stanley Kramer. Screenplay by John Paxton from the novel by Nevil Shute. Art director: Fernando Carrere. Running time: 133 minutes.

WITH Gregory Peck, Ava Gardner, Anthony Perkins, and Donna Anderson.
ASTAIRE's first dramatic role, in which he plays a nuclear scientist – one of the survivors of an atomic holocaust in a world which is coming to an end.

THE PLEASURE OF HIS COMPANY
Paramount Pictures 1961
Technicolor

Produced by William Perlberg. Directed by George Seaton. Music directed by Alfred Newman. Screenplay by Samuel Taylor from a play by Cornelia Otis Skinner and Samuel Taylor. Art directors: Hal Pereira and Tambi Larsen. Running time: 114 minutes.

WITH Debbie Reynolds, Lilli Palmer, Tab Hunter, and Gary Merrill.
ASTAIRE is a long-lost father who returns on the eve of his daughter's wedding and attempts to prevent the marriage. Having failed, he leaves with the Chinese cook instead.
HIS MUSICAL NUMBER: 'Lover' (Richard Rodgers and Lorenz Hart) song.

On the Beach

Silk Stockings

The Pleasure of His Company

THE NOTORIOUS LANDLADY
Columbia Pictures 1962

Produced by Fred Kohlmar. Directed by Richard Quine. Music directed by George Duning. Screenplay by Larry Gelbart and Blake Edwards from a novel by Margery Sharp. Art director: Cary Odell. Running time: 123 minutes.

WITH Kim Novak, Jack Lemmon, Lionel Jeffries, and Estelle Winwood.
ASTAIRE in a minor role as a diplomat, one of whose subordinates, Lemmon, is involved in a mysterious murder.

FINIAN'S RAINBOW
Warner Brothers 1968
Technicolor

Produced by Joseph Landon. Directed by Francis Ford Coppola. Music directed by Ray Heindorf. Screenplay by E. Y. Harburg and Fred Saidy from their stage musical. Lyrics by E. Y. Harburg. Music by Burton Lane. Dance director: Hermes Pan. Art director: Hilyard M. Brown. Running time: 145 minutes.

WITH Petula Clark, Tommy Steele, Don Francks, and Keenan Wynn.
ASTAIRE is an Irish immigrant pursued to Fort Knox by a leprechaun whose crock of gold he has stolen.
HIS MUSICAL NUMBERS: 'Look to the Rainbow' song with Clark; dance. 'If This Isn't Love' song with Francks, Clark, and chorus; dance. 'When the Idle Poor Become the Idle Rich' song and dance with chorus.

THE MIDAS RUN
GB: A RUN ON GOLD
Selmur Pictures 1969
Technicolor

Produced by Raymond Stross. Directed by Alf Kjellin. Screenplay by James Buchanan and Ronald Austin from a story by Berne Giler. Art directors: Arthur Lawson and Ezio Cescotti. Running time: 106 minutes.

WITH Anne Heywood, Richard Crenna, Roddy McDowell, Sir Ralph Richardson, and Cesar Romero. Also features Fred Astaire Jr.
ASTAIRE plays a senior British secret agent who masterminds a bullion robbery and is then assigned the task of catching the hi-jackers.

THAT'S ENTERTAINMENT
Metro–Goldwyn–Mayer 1974
Metrocolor

Produced, directed and compiled by Jack Haley Jr. A compilation movie retelling the history of the MGM musical from the beginning of the Talkies to the mid 1950s. Running time: 137 minutes

WITH all MGM's greatest musical stars, and co-presenters Bing Crosby, Gene Kelly, Peter Lawford, Liza Minnelli, Donald O'Connor, Debbie Reynolds, Mickey Rooney, Frank Sinatra, James Stewart, and Liz Taylor.
ASTAIRE appears in several of the film clips and as a host-presenter.
HIS MUSICAL NUMBERS: 'Begin the Beguine', 'They Can't Take That Away From Me', 'Rhythm of the Day', 'I Guess I'll Have to Change My Plan', 'Hat Rack Dance', 'Shoes With Wings On', 'You're All the World to Me', 'Dancing in the Dark', and 'By Myself'.

That's Entertainment

Finian's Rainbow

The Notorious Landlady

The Midas Run

167

THE TOWERING INFERNO
Twentieth Century–Fox / Warner 1975
Colour

Produced by Irwin Allen. Directed by John Guillermin. Screenplay by Stirling Silliphant. Art director: Ward Preston. Running time: 165 minutes.

WITH Steve McQueen, Paul Newman, William Holden, Faye Dunaway, Susan Blakely, Richard Chamberlain, Jennifer Jones, O. J. Simpson, Robert Vaughn, and Robert Wagner.
ASTAIRE is a confidence trickster, one of the guests trapped by fire in the world's tallest skyscraper.

THAT'S ENTERTAINMENT PART 2
Metro–Goldwyn–Mayer 1976
Metrocolor

Produced by Saul Chaplin and Daniel Melnick. A second compilation movie with more extracts from MGM's musicals, a number of non-musical clips, and some original musical sequences. Narration by Leonard Gersche. Special lyrics by Howard Dietz and Saul Chaplin. Music arranged and conducted by Nelson Riddle. Dance director: Gene Kelly. Running time: 133 minutes.

WITH many of MGM's great musical and non-musical stars, and co-presenter Gene Kelly.
ASTAIRE appears in several of the film clips, with Kelly in four new sequences, and as a host-presenter.
HIS MUSICAL NUMBERS: (film clips) 'That's Entertainment', 'I Wanna Be a Dancing Man', 'I Love All of You', 'Easter Parade', 'Three Little Words', 'Triplets', 'Steppin' Out with My Baby', 'A Couple of Swells', and 'Bouncing the Blues'; (new numbers) 'That's Entertainment Part 2', 'Be a Clown', 'Shubert Alley', and 'Cartoon Sequence'.

The Towering Inferno

That's Entertainment Part 2

THE AMAZING DOBERMANS
Golden Films 1976
Colour

Produced by David Chudnow. Directed by Byron Chudnow. Screenplay by Richard Chapman from a story by Michael Kariake and William Goldstein. Running time: 96 minutes.

WITH James Franciscus, Barbara Eden, Jack Carter, Charlie Bill, James Almanzar, and Billy Barty.
ASTAIRE is the bible-toting, reformed conman owner of the said hounds, who befriends Franciscus, an undercover agent for the Justice Department, joins a circus with an amazing dog act, and helps catch a gambling and extortion racketeer.

UN TAXI MAUVE
Sofracima / Rizzoli Films 1977
Eastmancolor

Produced by Catherine Winter and Gisèle Rebillion. Directed by Yves Boisset, who also wrote the screenplay from the novel by Michel Deon. Music by Philippe Sarde. Art director: Arrigo Equini. Running time: 120 minutes.

WITH Charlotte Rampling, Philippe Noiret, Agostina Belli, Peter Ustinov, and Edward Albert Jr.
ASTAIRE plays Dr Scully, a 'philosophical' Irish country doctor, who numbers amongst his patients several rich and/or beautiful people trying to escape their problems.

Un Taxi Mauve

The Amazing Dobermans

DISCOGRAPHY

The abbreviations used are as follows: E.Col. for English Columbia, WRC for World Record Club, M–E for Monmouth–Evergreen, Br. for Brunswick, and Voc. for Vocalion. 78 & 45 rpm record numbers appear in Roman type; $33\frac{1}{3}$ rpm record number in italics. An asterisk ★ indicates a dance solo.

1923
THE WHICHNESS OF THE WHATNESS
OH, GEE! OH, GOSH!
vocals with Adele Astaire
HMV B1719/*WRC 125*; *M–E 7037*

1926
FASCINATING RHYTHM
vocal with Adele Astaire
THE HALF OF IT, DEARIE, BLUES★
George Gershwin, piano
E.Col. 3969/*WRC 124*; *M–E 7036*
HANG ON TO ME
I'D RATHER CHARLESTON
vocals with Adele Astaire
George Gershwin, piano
E.Col. 3970/*WRC 124*; *M–E 7036*
SWISS MISS
vocal with Adele Astaire
E.Col. 3979/*WRC 124*; *M–E 7036*

1928
HIGH HAT
MY ONE AND ONLY★
E. Col. 5173/*WRC 125*; *M–E 7037*
FUNNY FACE
THE BABBITT AND THE BROMIDE
vocals with Adele Astaire
E.Col. 5174/*WRC 125*; *M–E 7037*

1929
NOT MY GIRL
LOUISIANA
Al Starita Orchestra
E.Col. 5355/*WRC 124*; *M–E 7036*

1930
PUTTIN' ON THE RITZ★
CRAZY FEET★
E.Col. DB96/*WRC 124*; *M–E 7036*

1931
I LOVE LOUISA
NEW SUN IN THE SKY
Leo Reisman Orchestra
Victor 22755/*Vik 1001*
WHITE HEAT
HOOPS
vocals with Adele Astaire
Leo Reisman Orchestra
Victor 22836/*Vik 1001*; Side 2
also *RCA LPV 565*
THE BAND WAGON
Leo Reisman Orchestra
SWEET MUSIC
vocal with Adele Astaire
HOOPS
vocal with Adele Astaire
I LOVE LOUISA
WHITE HEAT
Arthur Schwartz, piano
Victor L 24003

1932
NIGHT AND DAY
I'VE GOT YOU ON MY MIND
Leo Reisman Orchestra
Victor 24193/*Vik 1001*; Eng.
RCA RD 7756; *RCA Intl. 1037*;
Side 1 also *RCA LPV 565*

1933
MAYBE I LOVE YOU TOO MUCH
Leo Reisman Orchestra
Victor 24262/*Vik 1001*; Eng.
RCA RD 7756; *RCA Intl. 1037*
GOLD DIGGER'S SONG
MY TEMPTATION
Leo Reisman Orchestra
Victor 24312/*Vik 1001*; Eng.
RCA RD 7756; *RCA Intl. 1037*;
Side 1 also *RCA LPV 565*
NIGHT AND DAY
AFTER YOU
E.Col. DB1215/*WRC 124*; *M–E 7036*
FLYING DOWN TO RIO
MUSIC MAKES ME★
Col. 2912D; E.Col. DB1329/*WRC 124*;
M–E 7036; Side 2 also *Epic L2N 6072*

A HEART OF STONE
Leo Reisman Orchestra
Victor 24358/*Vik 1001*; *Eng. RCA RD 7756*;
RCA Intl. 1037

1935
CHEEK TO CHEEK
NO STRINGS★
Leo Reisman Orchestra
Br. 7486/Side 1 also *Epic FLM 13103*;
Harmony 30549
ISN'T THIS A LOVELY DAY?
TOP HAT, WHITE TIE AND TAILS★
Johnny Green Orchestra
Br. 7487
THE PICCOLINO
Leo Reisman Orchestra
Br. 7488

1936
LET'S FACE THE MUSIC AND DANCE
LET YOURSELF GO★
Johnny Green Orchestra
Br. 7608
I'M PUTTING ALL MY EGGS IN ONE
    BASKET
WE SAW THE SEA
Johnny Green Orchestra
Br. 7609
I'D RATHER LEAD A BAND★
I'M BUILDING UP TO AN AWFUL LET-
    DOWN
Johnny Green Orchestra
Br. 7610; Col. 3118D
A FINE ROMANCE
Johnny Green Orchestra
Br. 7716/*Epic FLM 13103*
THE WAY YOU LOOK TONIGHT
PICK YOURSELF UP★
Johnny Green Orchestra
Br. 7717
NEVER GONNA DANCE
BOJANGLES OF HARLEM★
Johnny Green Orchestra
Br. 7718/Side 2 also *Epic L2N 6064*

1937
THEY CAN'T TAKE THAT AWAY FROM ME
(I'VE GOT) BEGINNER'S LUCK
Johnny Green Orchestra
Br. 7855/Side 1 also *Epic FLM 13103*
THEY ALL LAUGHED
SLAP THAT BASS★
Johnny Green Orchestra
Br. 7856/*Epic FLM 13103*; Side 2 *Epic FLM 15105*
LET'S CALL THE WHOLE THING OFF
SHALL WE DANCE?★
Johnny Green Orchestra
Br. 7857/Side 1 also *Epic FLM 13103*
A FOGGY DAY
I CAN'T BE BOTHERED NOW★
Ray Noble Orchestra
Br. 7982/*Epic FLM 13103*
THINGS ARE LOOKING UP
NICE WORK IF YOU CAN GET IT★
Ray Noble Orchestra
Br. 7983/*Epic FLM 13103*

1938
CHANGE PARTNERS
I USED TO BE COLOR BLIND
Ray Noble Orchestra
Br. 8189/Side 1 also *Epic FLM 13103*
THE YAM★
THE YAM STEP★
Ray Noble Orchestra
Br. 8190

1940
WHO CARES?
JUST LIKE TAKING CANDY FROM A
BABY★
Benny Goodman Orchestra
Col. 355517/*Col. CSM 891*
LOVE OF MY LIFE
ME AND THE GHOST UPSTAIRS★
orchestra conducted by Perry Botkin
Col. 35815
POOR MISTER CHISHOLM
(I AIN'T HEP TO THAT STEP BUT I'LL) DIG
    IT★
orchestra conducted by Perry Botkin
Col. 35852/Side 2 also *Epic FLM 13103*

1941
SO NEAR AND YET SO FAR
SINCE I KISSED MY BABY GOODBYE
vocal with Delta Rhythm Boys
orchestra conducted by Harry Sosnik
Decca 18187/Side 1 also *Voc. 3716*
DREAM DANCING
THE WEDDING CAKE-WALK
vocal with Delta Rhythm Boys
orchestra conducted by Harry Sosnik
Decca 18188/*Voc. 3716*

1942
I'LL CAPTURE YOUR HEART SINGING★
vocal with Bing Crosby, Margaret Lenhart
Bob Crosby Orchestra
Decca 18427/*Decca 4256*
YOU'RE EASY TO DANCE WITH
I CAN'T TELL A LIE
Decca 18428/*Decca 4256*; Side 1 also *Voc. 3716*
LET'S SAY IT WITH FIRECRACKERS★
Bob Crosby Orchestra
Decca (unissued)
YOU WERE NEVER LOVELIER
ON THE BEAM
orchestra conducted by John Scott Trotter
Decca 18489/*Voc. 3716*
I'M OLD FASHIONED
WEDDING IN THE SPRING
orchestra conducted by John Scott Trotter
Decca 18490/Side 1 also *Voc. 3716*
DEARLY BELOVED
THE SHORTY GEORGE
orchestra conducted by John Scott Trotter
Decca 18491/*Voc. 3716*

1944
THIS HEART OF MINE
IF SWING GOES, I GO TOO
orchestra conducted by Albert Sack
Decca 23388/*Voc. 3716*

1945
ONE FOR MY BABY
OH, MY ACHIN' BACK
orchestra conducted by Albert Sack
Decca (unissued)

1946
PUTTIN' ON THE RITZ
A COUPLE OF SONG AND DANCE MEN★
vocal with Bing Crosby
orchestra conducted by John Scott Trotter
Decca 23650/Side 1 also *Voc. 3716*; Side 2 also
Decca 4259

1948
EASTER PARADE
vocal with Judy Garland
MGM Orchestra conducted by Johnny Green
MGM 30185/*MGM E3227*; *Eng. MGM 2353 076*
A COUPLE OF SWELLS
I LOVE A PIANO
SNOOKY OOKUMS
WHEN THE MIDNIGHT CHOO-CHOO
   LEAVES FOR ALABAM'
vocals with Judy Garland
MGM Orchestra conducted by Johnny Green
MGM 30186/*MGM E3227*; *Eng. MGM 2353 076*
IT ONLY HAPPENS WHEN I DANCE WITH
   YOU
MGM Orchestra conducted by Johnny Green
MGM 30187/*MGM E3413*
STEPPIN' OUT WITH MY BABY
MGM Orchestra conducted by Johnny Green
MGM 30188/MGM E3227; *MGM E3413*;
Eng. MGM 2353 076

1949
YOU'D BE HARD TO REPLACE
MY ONE AND ONLY HIGHLAND FLING
vocal with Ginger Rogers
MGM Orchestra conducted by Lennie Hayton
MGM 50016/Side 1 also *MGM E3413*
THEY CAN'T TAKE THAT AWAY FROM
   ME
SHOES WITH WINGS ON★
MGM Orchestra conducted by Lennie Hayton
MGM 50017/*MGM E3413*

1950
WHERE DID YOU GET THAT GIRL?
vocal with Anita Ellis
MGM Orchestra conducted by André Previn
MGM 30239/*MGM 3768*; *Eng. MGM 2353 033*
NEVERTHELESS
vocal with Anita Ellis and Red Skelton
MGM Orchestra conducted by André Previn
MGM 30240/*MGM E3768*; *Eng. MGM 2353 033*
MY SUNNY TENNESSEE
SO LONG, OO-LONG
THREE LITTLE WORDS
vocals with Rek Skelton
MGM Orchestra conducted by André Previn
MGM 30241/*MGM E3768*; *Eng. MGM 2353 033*

1951
HOW COULD YOU BELIEVE ME WHEN I
   SAID I LOVE YOU WHEN YOU KNOW
   I'VE BEEN A LIAR ALL MY LIFE?
vocal with Jane Powell
MGM Orchestra conducted by Johnny Green
MGM 30316/*MGM E3235*
I LEFT MY HAT IN HAITI
YOU'RE ALL THE WORLD TO ME
MGM Orchestra conducted by Johnny Green
MGM 30317/*MGM E3235*; Side 1 also
MGM E3413
EV'RY NIGHT AT SEVEN
MGM Orchestra conducted by Johnny Green
MGM 30319/*MGM E3235*; *MGM E3413*

1952
BABY DOLL
MGM Orchestra conducted by
Adolph Deutsch
MGM 30517/*MGM E3413*
OOPS!
SEEING'S BELIEVING
MGM Orchestra conducted by Adolph Deutsch
MGM 30518/Side 2 also *MGM E3413*
BACHELOR DINNER SONG
I WANNA BE A DANCIN' MAN★
MGM Orchestra conducted by Adolph Deutsch
MGM 30520
THE ASTAIRE STORY
Produced by Norman Granz
Oscar Peterson Group
ISN'T THIS A LOVELY DAY?†
PUTTIN' ON THE RITZ
I USED TO BE COLOR BLIND††
THE CONTINENTAL
LET'S CALL THE WHOLE THING OFF†
CHANGE PARTNERS†
'S WONDERFUL†
LOVELY TO LOOK AT
THEY ALL LAUGHED
CHEEK TO CHEEK
STEPPIN' OUT WITH MY BABY†
THE WAY YOU LOOK TONIGHT††
I'VE GOT MY EYES ON YOU
DANCING IN THE DARK
THE CARIOCA
NICE WORK IF YOU CAN GET IT
NEW SUN IN THE SKY††
I WON'T DANCE†
FAST DANCE★†
TOP HAT, WHITE TIE AND TAILS†
NO STRINGS
I CONCENTRATE ON YOU††
I'M PUTTING ALL MY EGGS IN ONE
   BASKET
A FINE ROMANCE†
NIGHT AND DAY†
FASCINATING RHYTHM
I LOVE LOUISA
SLOW DANCE★†
MEDIUM DANCE†
THEY CAN'T TAKE THAT AWAY FROM
   ME†
YOU'RE EASY TO DANCE WITH††
A NEEDLE IN A HAYSTACK

SO NEAR AND YET SO FAR††
A FOGGY DAY†
OH, LADY BE GOOD!
I'M BUILDING UP TO AN AWFUL LET-
    DOWN††
NOT MY GIRL
Clef MGC 101/2/3/4
†also *Verve MGV 2010*; ††also *Verve MGV 2114*

1953
A SHINE ON YOUR SHOES★
I LOVE LOUISA
MGM Orchestra conducted by Adolph Deutsch
MGM 30792/MGM E3051; MGM E3413
BY MYSELF
THAT'S ENTERTAINMENT
vocal with Nanette Fabray, Jack Buchanan, Oscar
Levant, and India Adams
MGM Orchestra conducted by Adolph Deutsch
MGM 30793/MGM E3051; Side 1 also
MGM E3413
TRIPLETS
vocal with Nanette Fabray and Jack Buchanan
MGM Orchestra conducted by Adolph Deutsch
MGM 30794/MGM E3051
I GUESS I'LL HAVE TO CHANGE MY PLAN
vocal with Jack Buchanan
MGM Orchestra conducted by Adolph Deutsch
MGM 30795/MGM E3051
THE BAND WAGON *film soundtrack*
MGM Orchestra conducted by Adolph Deutsch
THE GIRL HUNT BALLET
narrated by Fred Astaire
plus vocals above also recorded on 78 rpm
MGM E3051

1955
SOMETHING'S GOTTA GIVE
SLUEFOOT
orchestra conducted by Russ Garcia
RCA Victor 20-6140/Side 1
also *Reader's Digest 49-5*

1956
HELLO, BABY
THERE'S NO TIME LIKE THE PRESENT
Buddy Bregman Orchestra
Verve 2009/Verve MGV 2114
SWEET SORROW
JUST LIKE TAKING CANDY FROM A BABY
Buddy Bregman Orchestra
Verve 2019/Verve MGV 2114
CLAP YO' HANDS★
vocal with Kay Thompson
orchestra conducted by Adolph Deutsch
Verve 10041X45/Verve MGV 15001
HE LOVES AND SHE LOVES
FUNNY FACE★
orchestra conducted by Adolph Deutsch
Verve 10042X45/Verve MGV 15001
FUNNY FACE *film soundtrack*
orchestra conducted by Adolph Deutsch
FUNNY FACE★
BONJOURS, PARIS!
vocal with Audrey Hepburn and Kay Thompson
CLAP YO' HANDS★
vocal with Kay Thompson

HE LOVES AND SHE LOVES
LET'S KISS AND MAKE UP
'S WONDERFUL
vocal with Audrey Hepburn
Verve MGV 15001

1957
THAT FACE
CALYPSO HOORAY
Buddy Bregman Orchestra
Verve 10051X45/Side 1 also *Verve MGV 2114*
SILK STOCKINGS *film soundtrack*
MGM Orchestra conducted by André Previn
TOO BAD
vocal with Peter Lorre, Joseph Buloff, and Jules
Munshin
PARIS LOVES LOVERS
vocal with Carol Richards
STEREOPHONIC SOUND
vocal with Janis Paige
ALL OF YOU
FATED TO BE MATED
THE RITZ ROLL AND ROCK
MGM E3542ST/Eng. MGM 2353 034

1959
I'LL WALK ALONE
THE AFTERBEAT
orchestra conducted by Pete King
Kapp 311X
THAT FACE
THANK YOU SO MUCH, MISSUS
    LOWSBOROUGH-GOODBY
orchestra conducted by David Rose
Choreo 100/Choreo A-1
NOW
orchestra conducted by Pete King
CHANGE PARTNERS
ISN'T THIS A LOVELY DAY?
A FOGGY DAY
THE GIRL ON THE MAGAZINE COVER
I LOVE TO QUARREL WITH YOU
ALONG CAME RUTH
THE AFTERBEAT
THEY CAN'T TAKE THAT AWAY FROM
    ME
THEY ALL LAUGHED
I'LL WALK ALONE
ONE FOR MY BABY
OH, LADY BE GOOD!
PUTTIN' ON THE RITZ
TOP HAT, WHITE TIE AND TAILS
LADY OF THE EVENING
SOMETHING'S GOTTA GIVE
Kapp KL 1165/KS 3049

1960
**THREE EVENINGS WITH FRED
ASTAIRE** *TV soundtrack*
orchestra conducted by David Rose
OH, LADY BE GOOD
CHEEK TO CHEEK
A FINE ROMANCE
THEY CAN'T TAKE THAT AWAY FROM
    ME
NICE WORK IF YOU CAN GET IT
A FOGGY DAY

I WON'T DANCE
SOMETHING'S GOTTA GIVE
NIGHT AND DAY
TOP HAT, WHITE TIE AND TAILS
FASCINATING RHYTHM
DANCING IN THE DARK
THE WAY YOU LOOK TONIGHT
DEARLY BELOVED
STEPPIN' OUT WITH MY BABY
LET'S FACE THE MUSIC AND DANCE
THE CARIOCA
THE CONTINENTAL
ONE FOR MY BABY
BY MYSELF
THAT FACE
MISS OTIS REGRETS
THANK YOU SO MUCH, MISSUS
    LOWSBOROUGH-GOODBY
FUNNY FACE
I LOVE LOUISA
FLYING DOWN TO RIO
I'M PUTTING ALL MY EGGS IN ONE
    BASKET
THEY ALL LAUGHED
LOVELY TO LOOK AT
LET'S CALL THE WHOLE THING OFF
EASTER PARADE
A SHINE ON YOUR SHOES
Choreo A-1

1962

THE NOTORIOUS LANDLADY
THE MARTINI
orchestra conducted by Dick Hazard
Choreo 104
IT HAPPENS EVERY SPRING
YOU WORRY ME
orchestra conducted by Dick Hazard
Ava 125

1968

FINIAN'S RAINBOW *film soundtrack*
orchestra conducted by Ray Heindorf
LOOK TO THE RAINBOW
vocal with Petula Clark
IF THIS ISN'T LOVE
vocal with Don Francks and Petula Clark
WHEN THE IDLE POOR BECOME THE
    IDLE RICH
vocal with Petula Clark
Warner BS2550

1971

**'S WONDERFUL, 'S MARVELOUS,
'S GERSHWIN** *TV soundtrack*
orchestra conducted by Elliot Lawrence
'S WONDERFUL
OH, LADY BE GOOD!
THEY ALL LAUGHED
FASCINATING RHYTHM
A FOGGY DAY
LET'S CALL THE WHOLE THING OFF
THEY CAN'T TAKE THAT AWAY FROM
    ME
Daybreak 2009

1974

STARRING FRED ASTAIRE
CHEEK TO CHEEK
NO STRINGS
ISN'T THIS A LOVELY DAY?
TOP HAT, WHITE TIE AND TAILS
THE PICCOLINO
LET'S FACE THE MUSIC AND DANCE
LET YOURSELF GO
I'M PUTTING ALL MY EGGS IN ONE
    BASKET
WE SAW THE SEA
I'D RATHER LEAD A BAND
I'M BUILDING UP TO AN AWFUL LET-
    DOWN
A FINE ROMANCE
THE WAY YOU LOOK TONIGHT
PICK YOURSELF UP
NEVER GONNA DANCE
BOJANGLES OF HARLEM
WALTZ IN SWING TIME
orchestral
THEY CAN'T TAKE THAT AWAY FROM
    ME
(I'VE GOT) BEGINNER'S LUCK
THEY ALL LAUGHED
SLAP THAT BASS
LET'S CALL THE WHOLE THING OFF
SHALL WE DANCE?
A FOGGY DAY
I CAN'T BE BOTHERED NOW
THINGS ARE LOOKING UP
NICE WORK IF YOU CAN GET IT
CHANGE PARTNERS
I USED TO BE COLOR BLIND
THE YAM
THE YAM STEP
special 2-record LP collection of all Brunswick
releases, 1935-38
Columbia SG32472/CBS 88062

1978

THE BELLE OF NEW YORK *film soundtrack*
MGM Orchestra conducted by Adolph Deutsch
WHEN I'M OUT WITH THE BELLE OF
    NEW YORK
BACHELOR DINNER SONG
SEEING'S BELIEVING
OOPS!
I WANNA BE A DANCIN' MAN
Buddy Bregman Orchestra
THERE'S NO TIME LIKE THE PRESENT
JUST LIKE TAKING CANDY FROM A BABY
HELLO BABY
SWEET SORROW
Dick Hazard Orchestra
THE MARTINI
IT HAPPENS EVERY SPRING
YOU WORRY ME
THE NOTORIOUS LANDLADY
Stet DS 15004
THE ASTAIRE STORY
reissue (see 1952 for details)
DRG DARC-3-1102

Acknowledgments

Publications

Grateful acknowledgment is made to the critics, authors, journalists and songwriters who are quoted in this book – and also to their publishers. 'You're the Top' from 'Anything Goes' (words and music by Cole Porter) is © 1934 Harms Inc. (Warner Bros); the title song from 'On Your Toes' (words by Lorenz Hart and music by Richard Rodgers) is © 1936 Chappell & Co., Inc; 'Do It the Hard Way' from 'Pal Joey' (words by Lorenz Hart and music by Richard Rodgers) is © 1940 Chappell & Co., Inc. All three are reproduced by kind permission of Chappell & Co. Ltd, 50 New Bond Street, London W1A 2BR.

Astaire, Fred: *Steps in Time*. Harper and Row, New York, 1959. William Heinemann, London, 1960.

Cooke, Alistair (editor): *Garbo and the Night Watchman*. Originally published 1937. Secker and Warburg, London, 1971. McGraw–Hill, New York, 1972.

Croce, Arlene: *After Images*. Random House, New York, 1977.

Croce, Arlene: *The Fred Astaire and Ginger Rogers Book*. Outerbridge and Lazard Inc., New York, and W. H. Allen, London, 1972.

Dietz, Howard: *Dancing in the Dark*. Bantam Books, Illinois, 1974 and London, 1976.

Fitzgerald, F. Scott: *The Great Gatsby*. Originally published 1920. Penguin, London, 1969. Scribner's, New York, 1978.

Gershwin, Ira: *Lyrics on Several Occasions*. Viking Press, New York, 1973.

Green, Stanley and Burt Goldblatt: *Starring Fred Astaire*. Dodd, Mead and Co., New York, 1973. W. H. Allen, London, 1974.

Greene, Graham: *The Pleasure Dome*. Secker and Warburg, London, 1972.

Higham, Charles: *Ziegfeld*. W. H. Allen, London, 1973.

Kael, Pauline: *Deeper Into Movies*. Little, Brown and Co., Massachusetts, 1973. Calder and Boyars, London, 1975.

Kael, Pauline: *Reeling*. Little, Brown and Co., Massachusetts, 1976. M. Boyars, London, 1977.

Lerner, Alan Jay: *The Street Where I Live*. W. W. Norton, New York, 1978.

Wilson, Edmund: *Classics and Commercials*. Farrar, Straus and Giroux, New York, 1950.

Wodehouse, P. G.: *A Damsel in Distress*. Originally published 1919. British Book Centre, New York, 1956. Star Books, London, 1978.

Photographs

Colour photographs: British Film Institute, London 63 bottom, 97 top, 98 inset, 133, 136; Cinema Bookshop, London 62, 97 bottom; Frank Driggs Collection, New York 26 bottom left and bottom right; Film Pictorial 61; Ken Galante, New York 100; Lester Glassner Collection, New York 27; Ronald Grant, Cambridge 63 top; Kobal Collection, London 64; The Raymond Mander and Joe Mitchenson Theatre Collection, London 25, 26 top left and top right; Popperfoto, London 134, 135; Radio Times, London 28, 98–9.

Black and white photographs: B.C.W. Publishing, Ryde 168 top right; Bettmann Archive, New York 7, 9 top and bottom, 36, 38, 44, 50, 144, 145, 146 top and bottom, 147 top and bottom, 148 top and bottom; British Film Institute, London half-title page, 6, 60, 65 top and bottom, 73 bottom, 78 top and bottom, 87, 88 bottom, 96, 105 top, 108 bottom right, 113, 117, 120, 121, 123 top left, 125 top, 129, 131 top left, 137, 142 top, 149, 156 left, 157 bottom right, 158 left and right, 159 lower right, 160 right, 161 left and bottom right, 162 top left and right, 163 top left and bottom left, 164 top, bottom left and bottom right, 165 top right and bottom right, 166 top, bottom left and bottom right, 167 bottom right, 169; Cinema Bookshop, London title page, 53, 67, 73 top, 77 top left and right, 88 top, 89 bottom, 94, 110 bottom, 115 top left, 122, 124, 130, 141, 143, 159 bottom left, 162 bottom left; Culver Pictures, New York 8 top, 12, 13, 15 bottom, 33 bottom, 42, 45 bottom, 68 top, 86 top, 153, 153 inset; Frank Driggs Collection, New York 15 top; Joel Finler, London 80 top and bottom, 168 bottom left; Lester Glassner Collection, New York 8 bottom, 10, 14, 23, 32, 37 bottom, 40, 41, 43, 46 bottom, 47, 152; Ronald Grant, Cambridge 55 top, 91 top left, 139, 168 top left; Hamlyn Group Picture Library contents spread, 95; Kobal Collection, London endpapers, 54, 55 bottom, 56, 57 bottom, 58 top and bottom left, 59, 68 bottom, 68–9, 70, 75, 76, 77 bottom left, 80–1, 83, 84, 85, 89 top, 90, 91 top right and bottom, 92, 93, 101, 102, 103 top, centre and bottom, 106, 107, 108 top and bottom left, 109, 110 top, 111, 112, 114, 115 top right and bottom, 116, 118, 119 top and bottom, 123 top right and bottom, 125 bottom left and bottom right, 126 top, centre and bottom, 127, 128, 131 top right and bottom, 156 right, 158 bottom right, 159 top right, 160 bottom left, 161 top right, 165 left, 167 top right; The Raymond Mander and Joe Mitchenson Theatre Collection, London 13 inset, 16, 17 left and right, 18 top, 19, 30–1, 33 top, 34–5, 35 top and bottom, 39 top left, 154, 157 left; Movie Star News, New York 82, 132, 167 left, 168 bottom right; Penguin Photo, New York 71 top left, top right and bottom; Pictorial Parade, New York 46 top; Pictorial Press, London 104, 150; Picturegoer, London 163 right; Popperfoto, London 57 top, 58 bottom right, 66, 72, 79, 86 bottom, 105 bottom, 142 bottom, 157 top right, 160 top left; Radio Times Hulton Picture Library, London 18 bottom, 39 top right and bottom, 49; Theatre World 48; United Press International, New York 37 top, 51; Victoria and Albert Museum, London 21; Warner-Pathé 138 bottom, 167 centre right; Wide World Photos, New York 45 top.

US research by Research Reports, New York.

Index

Figures in italics refer to captions